WILD LEARNING

WILD LEARNING

PRACTICAL IDEAS TO BRING TEACHING OUTDOORS

Rachel Tidd

JB JOSSEY-BASS™

A Wiley Brand

Published by John Wiley & Sons, Inc., Hoboken, New Jersey.
Published simultaneously in Canada.

ISBNs: 9781119931348 (paperback), 9781119931331 (ePDF), 9781119931324 (ePub)

For general information on our other products and services or for technical support, please contact our Customer Care Department within the United States at (800) 762-2974, outside the United States at (317) 572-3993 or fax (317) 572-4002.

Wiley also publishes its books in a variety of electronic formats. Some content that appears in print may not be available in electronic formats. For more information about Wiley products, visit our web site at www.wiley.com.

Library of Congress Control Number:
2023000522 (print), 2023000523 (ebook)

Cover Design: Wiley
Cover Images: Floral frame: © Maria_Galybina/Getty Images
            Photo: © jacoblund/Getty Images

To my husband, Leo, for always believing in me and to my boys,
Finn and Taro, for inspiring me to bring teaching outside.

Contents

INTRODUCTION 1
- Benefits of teaching outdoors 1
- Zones of accessibility 4

01 Planning and preparation 13
- A place to gather 13
- Safety considerations 17
- Getting parents on board with outdoor learning 19
- Planning classroom outdoor time and classroom management 19
- Dressing for the weather: Gear for kids and adults 21
- Creating a positive outdoor experience for students and teachers 29
- Materials for outdoor learning 30
- Final thoughts 33

02 Lessons in the schoolyard 34
- The wonders of chalk 34
- Learning games for the schoolyard 51
- Using natural materials 68
- Utilizing the schoolyard 93
- Final thoughts 104

03 Visiting the neighborhood 105
- Walking adventures 106
- Final thoughts 149

04 Exploring farther afield 150
- The plants and animals around us 150
- Developing a sit spot practice 189
- Final thoughts 196

05 Inviting nature indoors 197
- A nature-inspired class meeting 197
- Cultivating nature appreciation and curiosity throughout the year 204
- Final thoughts 217

ACKNOWLEDGMENTS 219

ABOUT THE WEBSITE 220

INDEX 221

Introduction

Anything you teach in an indoor classroom can be taught outdoors, often in ways that are more enjoyable for children.

– Cathy James

This book, *Wild Learning*, came from my desire to help make outdoor learning and teaching more manageable and accessible to educators. The lessons and activities show you how to teach core subjects, in outdoor spaces such as the schoolyard and the neighborhood, as well as places farther afield. I want you to see the outdoors as a resource that can be used to teach your regular curriculum, not another extra subject or special event to try and fit into your day. For this reason, *Wild Learning* provides a collection of practical activities, projects, and classroom routines centered around math, reading, and writing.

Why outdoors? Because the outdoor environment provides so many benefits for you and your students! The outdoors provides a naturally multisensory learning environment and more opportunities for hands-on learning (often without extra planning!). Compared to being inside, outdoor learning increases student engagement and attention, supports mental and physical health, and helps children form a deeper connection with the natural world. These are outcomes we all want to optimize in our classrooms!

You can implement the lessons and activities in this book from your classroom right away, as the activities require no additional training or special materials. Your students will gain the benefits of outdoor learning by writing descriptive stories based on observations of cloud formations, collecting bundles of sticks to learn place value, using chalk to play word games on pavement, looking for geometry in nature and the built environment, and writing an ode to something in the neighborhood (see Figure 0.1).

Benefits of Teaching Outdoors

Simply moving instruction outdoors is healthier, helps children form a strong connection with the natural world, supports a variety of learning styles, increases engagement, and increases students' motivation to learn.[1] In addition, the mental health benefits of outdoor learning, such

Figure 0.1 Students working on a writing project outdoors
Source: Rachel Tidd

as reducing anxiety and depression, lowering stress, and improving self-confidence, have been well documented.[2] Schools continue to struggle to meet their students' learning and mental health needs. Incorporating more outdoor learning in schools is a simple and cost-effective way to support your students' social-emotional needs, learning styles, and increased engagement (see Figure 0.2).

The benefits of outdoor learning have even been shown to extend beyond a single outdoor lesson or activity. Some people mistakenly believe that the outdoor environment can be a distraction. However, a recent study has shown that taking lessons outside can positively affect student attention and engagement that lasts into the next lesson, even if the subsequent lesson is indoors.[3] The positive effects were seen even if only the location of the lesson changed, not the content or delivery method. This means that even small changes, such as teaching an indoor lesson outside, reading aloud outside, or conducting a writing lesson outdoors, can help improve students' attention and engagement for the following lesson, even if instruction moves back indoors (see Figure 0.3)!

Figure 0.2 Students exploring the area near their school
Source: Rachel Tidd

Figure 0.3 Students working in the schoolyard
Source: Mary Taylor / Pexels

Outdoor learning has also been shown to increase school achievement. Studies have shown an increase in standardized test scores, attendance, attitude about school, and improvements in behavior.[4] This is partially attributed to the multisensory and hands-on learning opportunities that learning outdoors typically provides. For example, practicing place value using bundles of sticks or making and writing words using word boxes drawn on the pavement.

Today's outdoor educational programs and curricula primarily focus on school gardens, the environment, science, or physical education. These programs are excellent, and if you have them at your school, take advantage of them! However, the reality is that for most teachers, special programs, training, and resources such as these are not available. The activities in this book are not trying to replace these outdoor programs, nor am I suggesting a completely outdoor program as with the forest school model.[4] The goal here is to provide regular classroom teachers like you with the tools and encouragement to teach portions of your core curriculum outdoors. The lessons and activities found in *Wild Learning* are designed to be low or no cost, require no special training, and are taught in common outdoor areas such as the schoolyard.

Zones of Accessibility

One advantage of outdoor learning is that it is a resource available to schools everywhere, and making it easier for teachers and schools to implement is an important goal of this book. The lessons and activities are organized around three outdoor areas accessible to teachers. The locations radiate from the school forming "zones" of accessibility (see Figure 0.4). The most accessible outdoor zone is the schoolyard, followed by the neighborhood surrounding the school, and finally, locations that are farther away and take more planning such as local parks and natural areas. These three types of outdoor spaces are generally available regardless of whether a school is in an urban, suburban, or rural setting. While schools in rural and suburban settings may have more extensive school grounds, urban schools typically have some outdoor space available and have more learning opportunities in the neighborhood surrounding the school. Still, some schools may find themselves confined to the schoolyard for safety reasons or school policies. Organizing activities by location enables you to select activities that work best for your school's setting, schedule, and resources.

In the schoolyard

The schoolyard is the most accessible of the three outdoor location types. For the purposes of this book, the schoolyard is defined as any

Zones of Accessibility

Figure 0.4 Zones of accessibility for outdoor learning surrounding a typical school
Source: Julie Manners. Inspiring / Shutterstock.

outdoor space available to you and your students on school property. This could mean a paved area, open field, playground, or even a rooftop (see Figure 0.5). Many schools in urban areas have completely paved schoolyards. This does not mean you cannot incorporate outdoor learning into your classroom! Chapter 3, In the Schoolyard, was written with this environment in mind. The chapter utilizes sidewalk chalk, learning games, natural materials, and playground equipment to fit any available space.

Just because an area in the schoolyard has not been used for instructional purposes before does not mean the space is not suitable! There is a huge opportunity to get creative and try new locations for learning. Elementary schools in Ithaca, New York, asked local landscaping

Figure 0.5 Students writing at a picnic table
Source: Rachel Tidd

companies to donate tree stumps to expand outdoor learning areas during the COVID-19 pandemic (see Figure 0.6). Many of these previously over-looked areas were in slivers of grass between the sidewalk and the school or schoolyard.[5] Getting students outside, even in highly urban areas, pro-vides significant mental, physical, and learning benefits to students even if the outdoor space is an urbanized environment (see Figure 0.7).

Visiting the neighborhood

The neighborhood around a school is often overlooked as a location where outdoor learning can take place. Yet, it is highly accessible to teachers, requires no transportation, and often can provide opportunities for community projects and involvement. For the purposes of this book, the school neighborhood is anywhere within a 10- to 30-minute walk

Figure 0.6 Tree stumps set up on school grounds for an outdoor
classroom in Ithaca, New York
Source: Rachel Tidd

Figure 0.7 This prekindergarten class at P.S. 185 – The Locke
School of Arts & Engineering in Harlem, New York,
moved the main areas of their classroom outside to
the primarily paved schoolyard
Source: Teresa Bello

Figure 0.8 A class working on a project on the sidewalk
Source: Andrew Chiappetta

around the school. Chapter 4, Visiting the Neighborhood, shows you how to take your class out to explore the area surrounding your school, helping your students foster a stronger sense of place and belonging, as well as providing a wider variety of activities, experiences, natural resources, and settings not available in the schoolyard (see Figure 0.8). Students will observe their neighborhood through a whole new lens through activities such as having students inventory tree species in the neighborhood or recording different examples of 2D and 3D shapes.

Exploring locations farther afield

For most schools, resources such as parks and natural areas are typically located outside the neighborhood zone (see Figure 0.9). These locations usually require more planning, transportation, and adult chaperones or additional staff. These requirements can act as barriers to visiting these

Figure 0.9 Students headed to explore a nature preserve
Source: Rachel Tidd

types of areas frequently. Visiting these special places provides students with immersive experiences in nature and fosters a deeper connection to the natural world. Chapter 5, Exploring Farther Afield, will show you ways to use these natural areas with activities and lessons that reinforce academic skills and expand students' knowledge about the natural world (see Figure 0.10).

Inviting nature indoors

While teaching core lessons outdoors is the primary focus of this book, the focus of chapter 6 is on inviting nature into your indoor classroom. Bringing nature into your classroom will help children extend and build enthusiasm for learning outdoors. Incorporating seasonal rhythms, nature observations, and nature-inspired routines into the classroom will foster a class culture that encourages careful observation and values the natural world.

Figure 0.10 Students from P.S. 146 – The Brooklyn New School,
visit the Brooklyn Bridge as part of their study
of bridges
Source: Andrew Chiappetta

For students who lack experience and/or may have fears associated with
the outdoors, building knowledge and familiarity with nature inside is the
first step to feeling comfortable outside.

Embracing the wild

Incorporating outdoor learning into the regular curriculum provides a
low-cost and effective way to increase student achievement and engagement, as well as improve student social-emotional and physical health. I
hope that this book will provide teachers at all types of schools with the
knowledge, strategies, and practical ideas to begin taking their teaching
practice outdoors (see Figures 0.11 and 0.12).

Figure 0.11 Students painting scenes from a story outdoors
Source: Rachel Tidd

Figure 0.12 Leaves make great surfaces for writing
Source: Rachel Tidd

Notes

1. J. Mann, T. Gray, S. Truong, E. Brymer, R. Passy, S. Ho, P. Sahlberg, K. Ward, P. Bentsen, C. Curry, and R. Cowper, "Getting Out of the Classroom and Into Nature: A Systematic Review of Nature-Specific Outdoor Learning on School Children's Learning and Development," *Frontiers in Public Health* 10 (2022), Article 877058, https://www.frontiersin.org/articles/10.3389/fpubh.2022.877058/full

2. K. Weir, "Nurtured by Nature," American Psychological Association, *Monitor on Psychology* (April 2020), https://www.apa.org/monitor/2020/04/nurtured-nature

3. M. Kuo, M. Browning, and M. Penner, "Do Lessons in Nature Boost Subsequent Classroom Engagement? Refueling Students in Flight," *Frontiers in Psychology* 8 (2018), Article 2253, https://www.frontiersin.org/articles/10.3389/fpsyg.2017.02253/full

4. The forest school model is a learner-led outdoor play and learning model that takes place in the forest or other natural environment. This is most commonly seen at the kindergarten or preschool level in the United States.

5. K. Langlois, "The Pandemic Moved Classrooms Outside: Let's Keep It That Way," *Outside* (August 2021), https://www.outsideonline.com/culture/active-families/covid-outdoor-learning-schools/

01 Planning and Preparation

Getting outside with your class is incredibly rewarding. You will likely notice that children are more engaged and excited to learn when you take them outdoors! Students who struggle indoors will often transform when engaged in outdoor learning – even becoming leaders. While transitioning to outdoor learning will take some practice (just like at the beginning of the school year when you teach classroom routines), you will likely find that student behavior improves!

In this chapter, you will find suggestions to help you plan, prepare, and be successful in teaching outdoors. You will find practical advice on choosing an outdoor area for your class to gather, suggested materials, classroom management tips, safety considerations, and sample schedules to help you prepare for learning outside. There is also a section devoted to explaining how to dress appropriately for different types of weather, ensuring you and your students will be comfortable and ready to learn.

A Place to Gather

The main outdoor classroom spaces used for lessons and activities in this book are the schoolyard, neighborhood, and natural areas farther afield. You don't need formal outdoor classroom space to teach outdoors! Outdoor learning can happen anywhere. Due to the short time periods and the way you will use outdoor classroom spaces, they do not need to be elaborate. For activities and lessons included in this book, you may only need a designated place to gather and give directions before heading out to the neighborhood or playing a game in the schoolyard. This outdoor meeting space can be as simple as sitting under the shade of a tree or on the steps of the school building. (See Figure 1.1.)

When choosing a suitable outdoor meeting area, consider noise or other distractions and take into account proximity to the playground as well as the availability of shade/shelter. Shade is important in warmer

Figure 1.1 Students using the steps of a church for writing in the neighborhood
Source: Rachel Tidd

weather or climates, while in winter you may wish to be in the sun or in a place that is sheltered from the wind (see Figure 1.2)! For this reason, you may need to change the meeting area location based on the seasons. Consider seating options, which can range from simply sitting on the grass or school steps to more elaborate setups such as tree stumps or benches.

Simple outdoor classroom spaces

Here are some locations you can consider for a simple outdoor classroom space: a shady spot under a tree, a corner of the schoolyard, rooftop outdoor spaces (common in urban schools), school garden, existing benches or picnic tables, stairs on the side or front of the school, sheltered side or corner of the school, outdoor lunch areas (when not in use), tennis or basketball courts (when not in use), and shared use spaces (some schools have agreements with city/town/churches on using spaces nearby the school). (See Figure 1.3.)

Simple ways to enhance or create an outdoor gathering space

You don't have to be limited by what is available in your outdoor space. There are many ways to enhance your outdoor area to make it more functional for learning outdoors. Here are some simple, inexpensive ways

Figure 1.2 Lesson under an awning at P.S. 185 in Harlem,
New York
Source: Teresa Bello

to enhance your space: add seating options, consider shelter, make areas for display and writing during whole group lessons or discussions, and make sure to have surfaces for students to write on.

Adding seating options such as log stumps, straw bales, or simple benches made from logs can be perfect solutions to providing seating on a small budget. Often landscape companies or parks departments will donate these for free (see Figure 1.4)! For waterproof seating that can go anywhere, consider inexpensive or donated yoga mats cut into squares, inexpensive garden kneeling pads, tarps, taking school chairs outside, or even plastic bucket covers. If your space needs shelter from the sun or rain, a large tarp and rope can be used to fashion a simple temporary shelter.

You will find it necessary at times to write and record ideas, concepts, and discussions; portable chalk or whiteboards are ideal for this purpose. Stringing ropes from trees or between poles from which to hang

Figure 1.3 Working outdoors on picnic tables
Source: Rachel Tidd

chart paper or clip things (number lines, timelines, etc.) can be a great alternative.

For individual student writing, a notebook can work well for writing outdoors. Clipboards can be great for holding and writing on worksheets outdoors. To keep these materials organized, consider finding a plastic crate or canvas bag to store and transport them. In the winter, laminated cardstock and dry-erase crayon/colored pencils work well as a waterproof writing surface.

If space and funds allow, larger additions to spaces such as hammocks for independent reading and writing, a covered outdoor library stocked with books, and a shed or other outdoor storage area to store supplies can be useful additions.

Before making even minor changes, reach out to other teachers, staff, administration, after-school programs, and other community members

Figure 1.4 Group work while sitting on log stump seats
Source: Rachel Tidd

about how the current schoolyard is used and identify the assets of the space, as well as any improvements that could be made. Including as many voices as possible in any discussions and planning will help bolster support for any proposed changes and minimize potential conflicts between different uses of the space. Consider and discuss how the area is used for recess, physical education classes, arrival/dismissal, fire drills, or by the community, and how any proposed additions or improvements may impact these uses.

Safety Considerations

Keeping students and staff safe in the outdoor learning environment is essential. Before embarking on an outdoor learning regime, discuss your plans with your principal or administrator. You can prepare for and mitigate potential risks by educating yourself and any additional staff, parent volunteers, and your students about potential risks. This will help everyone stay safe when learning and playing outdoors. Safety considerations, rules, and guidelines will vary according to your geographic location, setting, and school. Safety considerations and rules may need to change depending on where the class will be working each day. Before discussing safety considerations and guidelines with parents and students, spend time crafting a list of the most important considerations for your class.

Basic safety considerations

- Before taking your class outdoors, survey the school grounds for any potential hazards such as glass, garbage, suspicious persons, construction, etc.
- Always let the main office know when you take your class outside and where you will be, and take a cell phone or walkie-talkie with you.
- Obtain permission slips for walking field trips that cover the entire school year.
- Communicate to your students where they may explore and what the boundaries are when on school grounds, in the community, or in a natural area. Continue to survey the area when actively outside with your class for any emerging risks, such as weather.
- Before heading outside, review safety guidelines and rules that need to be followed.
- Become familiar with poisonous plants and plants that cause a reaction such as poison ivy. Learn how to identify them and teach your students and staff how to identify them.
- Learn about animals that may potentially be in the area and educate yourself, classroom staff, and your students about what to do if they come across any animals.
- Ask parents whether students have been stung by a bee and if there is any known reaction. Carry a list of students that have not been stung or have had a reaction. Discuss appropriate responses to bees, mosquitos, and other insects.
- Educate parents and students about how to dress for different types of weather (see the following section). Keep extra clothing in the classroom to lend if students are unprepared.
- Carry a small first aid kit.
- Bring plenty of water. Recycled gallon jugs work well for this purpose. Ask students to help carry them. They love being helpful!
- Determine the school's policy on applying sunscreen and bug spray if needed in your area. Do children bring and apply on their own? Do they apply before school? Are teachers allowed to apply it?

Getting Parents on Board with Outdoor Learning

Communicating with parents/guardians about the role and benefits of outdoor learning in your classroom and how they can help is essential to its success. Many teachers find it helpful to give examples of lessons, activities, or projects they plan on doing outdoors during an open house or meet the teacher night. This can also be a great time to discuss potential safety issues and how you plan on managing these concerns. Emphasize how the outdoor experiences enhance and support learning. Inviting parents to volunteer and help with outdoor activities and expeditions can help them see the benefits of learning outside firsthand and provide an extra pair of hands!

Consider incorporating information on your plans for outdoor learning in your welcome letter to parents/guardians, supply lists, and parent or open house nights at the beginning of the year. Being clear about any outdoor clothing needs, the frequency and schedule of outdoor experiences, and how they can support you will ensure the success of outdoor learning throughout the year. Make sure to mention if or how you can support families obtaining gear. (See "Making quality gear accessible for all" for ideas.) Sending a schedule and reminders home outlining any outdoor time or field trips planned each month can keep parents/guardians informed and help them prepare. Many teachers like to include this in their existing weekly or monthly newsletter to parents. Making outdoor learning time predictable and part of the weekly routine, such as devoting every Wednesday and Friday afternoon to outdoor lessons, can make it easier for parents and students to prepared with appropriate clothing and gear.

Planning Classroom Outdoor Time and Classroom Management

There are many ways to integrate outdoor learning time into your schedule. Making outdoor learning a part of the weekly routine can ensure your class gets outside regularly! Carving out consistent time(s) each week to take your class outside is the best way to ensure it happens.

If outdoor learning is new to you and your class, it may be best to start small. Choose one lesson or one morning/afternoon each week for outdoor learning. Focus your first outdoor lessons outdoors on introducing children to the new environment and the expectations. Just as we invest time in teaching classroom routines and expectations at the beginning of the school year, taking time to explain and practice the expectations for learning outside will set you and your students up for a success. You may want to focus initial lessons on getting to know the school grounds, learning how to interact respectfully with insects, identifying any plant or animal hazards, and reviewing rules and boundaries. Trying some easy, low-preparation activities such as read-alouds, free writes, independent reading, and games help students acclimate to the novelty of being outdoors before embarking on more in-depth projects and activities.

Outdoor classroom management tips

- Have students brainstorm a list of expectations for outdoor learning and the classroom. Record their answers on chart paper and revisit the list periodically.
- Discuss with students what they know and want to know about safety outdoors. This can be a great way to decide on any safety areas you may want or need to target with further instruction – for example, a mini-lesson on identifying poison ivy. Using a KWL (Know, Want to know, and Learned) chart to organize responses and track learning can be a great way to keep track of the discussion and learning.
- Consider assigning groups or partners before going outdoors. You can rotate groups monthly, quarterly, or any time that works best for your class.
- Follow a predictable routine each time you go out. This helps students know what to expect.
- Plan a loud signal for students to return after exploring or working on an activity. It might be a crow caw, howl, whistle, or phrase such as "circle up" or "all in!" Practice saying the signal and students responding.
- Use clipboards or notebooks to keep papers from flying away when working (see Figure 1.5).
- Use backpacks, bags, and/or bins devoted to outdoor learning to help keep materials ready and organized.

Figure 1.5 Students drawing trees in the neighborhood
Source: Andrew Chiappetta

Dressing for the Weather: Gear for Kids and Adults

There is no such thing as bad weather, only unsuitable clothing.

– Alfred Wainwright

While I agree with Alfred Wainwright's quote about the importance of outdoor clothing, everyone's personal level of comfort, school policies, resources, and weather challenges differ. There is no shame in rescheduling an outdoor lesson or day due to unusual or unsafe weather. Trying to learn or do an activity in a daylong rainstorm or heat wave without shelter can be downright unpleasant. Outdoor programs or schools that spend all

Sample Outdoor Class Schedules

While outdoor learning schedules can vary greatly, it is often helpful to see examples of how others have structured their time outdoors. Examples of single lessons, half-day, and full-day schedules are provided here.

Single lesson or activity

If you are only doing one lesson outdoors, a simple structure might be gathering for an explanation of the lesson/activity, sending students off to complete the activity, and then ending the activity by gathering again for a closing discussion.

Also, consider additional activities that could easily be done outdoors by themselves or following an outdoor lesson or activity to extend your time outdoors. Activities such as read-aloud time, independent reading, and morning meetings are often easily moved outdoors. Doing these activities requires minimal additional preparation or planning yet will help you and your students get more time outside and reduce time spent transitioning.

Half-day schedule

Planning to spend a half day outdoors is a great way to get started. It provides enough time for circle time, lessons, free play, and reflection.

- Circle time or game
- Lesson or activity
- Read-aloud
- Free play
- Ending circle or reflective discussion with journals

Full-day schedule

Your schedule may differ due to lunch times, specials, and the start and end times of your school day. This is meant to be a starting point to help you see how a day outside might look!

- Morning meeting
- Lesson or activity
- Read-aloud
- Game, lesson, or activity
- Lunch
- Free play
- Writing activity
- Closing circle
- Go inside to prep for dismissal

Outdoor Learning Tip: Move Independent Reading Outdoors

Taking independent reading time or read-alouds outdoors can be a simple way to get outside more with your class without planning a whole lesson (see Figure 1.6). Consider adding these activities to your regular outdoor learning time or scheduling one day a week where you plan to do them outside. Try bringing a book out to recess and before heading back inside, gather students and have your read-aloud outdoors!

Figure 1.6 Students listen to a read-aloud in the schoolyard at P.S. 185 in Harlem, New York
Source: Teresa Bello

day outside typically have various forms of shelter available, lots of gear, and can make a fire for warmth in very cold weather. Most teachers will not have these resources (at least initially!). Therefore, make decisions on the suitability and safety of weather conditions based on your situation.

If you and your students are new to outdoor learning, I suggest getting started when the weather is good and you and your students will not need extra gear. As you get more experienced with outdoor learning and begin to integrate it into your schedule regularly (and not just skip going out), you'll need to do some extra planning to determine appropriate gear requirements for your local climate.

Learning how to dress for various weather conditions can go a long way to making a variety of weather conditions suitable for outdoor learning (see Figure 1.7). It is essential to ensure that you, your students, and any staff or volunteers have appropriate gear for weather conditions typical for your geographic area.

Layers are key to adapting to changing conditions. Layers allow children and adults to adjust according to weather changes and activity levels (see Figure 1.8). Layers should be polyester, nylon, wool, or silk. Cotton absorbs moisture from sweat or weather conditions and draws heat from your body, making you cold. This can be dangerous in cold weather. Polyester and wool will keep you warm even if wet. Athletic clothing, fleece, and wool sweaters (some of the warmest are adult-sized sweaters that "shrunk" in the wash by accident) all make excellent layers. For more on layering, see the section "Layering Basics: three-layer rule for cold weather." Proper footwear for weather conditions is also essential. Depending on the conditions, children may need waterproof boots, warm boots, or sneakers.

Keep extra supplies in the classroom and bring extra mittens/gloves, hats, and socks outside with you. These are the most common clothing pieces that need to be replaced when they get wet through use or by accident. If students bring backpacks or bags, have them pack extra socks and mittens/gloves in the winter. Children should also have a complete change of clothes (including socks and underwear) and extra mittens/gloves/hats stored in the classroom. These extra clothes can be stored in cubbies, bags, clear plastic tubs (one for each child), or two-gallon reusable bags.

Layering basics: Three-layer rule for cold weather

The three-layer rule helps ensure you are dressed for any weather! It consists of three layers: the base layer, the insulating mid-layer, and the weatherproof outer layer (see Figure 1.9).

Outdoor Learning Tip: Making Quality Outdoor Gear Accessible for All

Quality outdoor gear can be expensive, and children can grow out of items quickly. Many schools have created outdoor gear libraries or hosted gear swaps to assist families in outfitting their children for outdoor learning. Gear libraries allow families to check out the outdoor gear they need for the school year and return it at the end. Families can donate outdoor clothes and gear in usable condition after their children have outgrown them to your classroom or the gear library. Fundraising and grant money can also be a way to add gear to the library. A simpler option is organizing a gear exchange. In a gear exchange, families bring gear they have outgrown and swap it for gear in the new size.

Figure 1.7 Rain pants and insulated boots are useful in many types of weather
Source: Rachel Tidd

Getting your class dressed and ready to go outside can take some time, especially when starting out. With time and practice, it will become easier and faster. Allow extra time before and after going outdoors for putting on and taking off all the outdoor gear in the winter. Younger students or those who need more support may benefit from visual checklists showing the clothing needed for the current season and the order it should be put on. Display the visual aid where students put on gear to help children be more independent with dressing. In the winter, to make dressing in layers more manageable and efficient in the classroom, consider asking parents to send students to school wearing their base layers on days you plan to spend a significant amount of time outdoors. They can bring regular clothes to change into afterward or remain in their base layers for the rest of the day.

Figure 1.8 Students dressed for winter weather
Source: Rachel Tidd

The 3 Layer Rule

1. Base Layer

Close-fitting synthetic or wool layers are key to staying warm in a variety of weather conditions.

2. Mid Layer

Fleece or wool makes an excellent mid layer. Add additional or thicker layers for the coldest temperatures. Optional in milder weather.

3. Weatherproof Layer

In wet weather, a raincoat and rain pants are essential. In cold weather, a warm jacket or parka and waterproof snow pants are best!

Figure 1.9 Layering infographic
Source: Design by Julie Manners, photos by Rachel Tidd

Layer 1: Base layer

Begin with the base layer, which should be close to the skin and made of polyester, fleece, or wool layers. This helps wick moisture from perspiration from skin, which can make you feel cold. Wool or synthetic socks are also important.

Layer 2: Insulating mid-layer

Next, add a mid-layer of fleece, wool, or other thicker non-cotton mid-weight layer. Fleece pants, jackets, and wool sweaters make great mid-weight layers. Extra wool socks are recommended for freezing weather.

Layer 3: The weatherproof outer layer

Finally, depending on the weather, add a raincoat and rain pants or snow pants and a winter jacket. Accessories such as neoprene rain boots, mittens or gloves, a hat, and a scarf or balaclava can be added.

Dressing for specific weather conditions

Choosing suitable clothing for the day's weather conditions can be tricky! Following are some guidelines to help you select clothing for more challenging weather.

Dressing for wet or rainy weather

A raincoat with a hood, rain pants, and rain or neoprene-insulated boots are essential to enjoying and learning in wet weather. Rain pant cuffs should go over the outside of boots. Layer as needed under rainwear. Polyester layers are best for milder temperatures. Umbrellas may also be helpful.

Dressing for very cold/dry weather (below 32°F or 0°C)

Layering is the key to being comfortable for long periods outdoors in cold weather. You can add more base or mid-layers for extremely cold weather. Make sure that mittens or gloves have cuffs that are long enough that they do not let snow in. Balaclavas, hats with ear flaps, or a hat under a hood can be helpful in windy conditions. Insulated snow boots are recommended for the coldest weather conditions.

Dressing for cold and wet conditions

Cold and wet conditions can be the most challenging to dress for. Again, follow the three-layer rule by adding layers as needed for the temperature. Then layer rain pants and a rain jacket with a hood on top of everything. Rain jackets can also be layered over a lightweight down or winter jacket to provide a waterproof outer layer. Having one to two extra pairs of waterproof mittens or gloves per student is recommended. Finish the outfit with insulated neoprene rain boots and wool socks. Regular rainboots are not recommended in these conditions because they are not warm enough.

Dressing for hot weather

Lightweight breathable clothing, sun hat, and closed-toe shoes or sandals are important for warm-weather adventures! Investigate your school's policy on sunscreen and bug spray application. You may need to obtain permission from parents to assist with the application or students may need to apply it themselves. Students should supply their own. It is a good idea to suggest that students apply sunscreen before coming to school. Umbrellas can also be useful for providing shade.

Creating a Positive Outdoor Experience for Students and Teachers

It is important to recognize that not all students and teachers will be comfortable with the outdoors. Students, teachers, and other community members may need support to feel welcome and safe while teaching and learning outside. Any fear of the outdoors harbored by a student will impact their learning. Therefore, teachers need to plan ways to make students feel welcome and safe when outside. Make sure to inform parents and students at the beginning of the year that you intend to incorporate outdoor learning throughout the year.

You can begin helping students feel more comfortable about the natural world by laying the groundwork for outdoor learning inside the classroom. A teacher's mindset and positive attitude significantly impact students' perceptions, sense of security, and attitude toward the outdoors.[1]

Using positive language to describe the outdoors and creating a classroom culture of curiosity about the natural world can make a big difference for students. Activities in chapter 6, Bringing Nature Inside, provide many suggestions to encourage students to observe and wonder about nature while indoors. These experiences can help students with little experience with being outdoors or in nature become more comfortable and gain knowledge about the outdoors in a safe space.

Reading picture and chapter books about nature or stories that involve nature can also help students learn more about the natural environment before or in conjunction with outdoor experiences. Educating students, parents, and teachers about common risks such as insect bites or plants such as poison ivy can help them feel more prepared and reduce anxiety when venturing outside. Lead discussions of their concerns about going outside and together brainstorm ways to deal with them. Try taking

Picture Books to Encourage a Positive Attitude About Going Outdoors

Run Wild by David Covell

Daniel Finds a Poem by Micha Archer

Fatima's Great Outdoors by Ambreen Tariq

Finding Wild by Megan Wagner Lloyd

Outside In by Deborah Underwood

Thunder Cake by Patricia Polacco

Scaredy Squirrel by Mélanie Watt

A Stick Is an Excellent Thing: Poems Celebrating Outdoor Play by Marilyn Singer

A Snowy Day by Ezra Jack Keats

And Then It's Spring by Julie Fogliano

short educational nature walks to show children things like poison ivy or to observe bee behavior. These real-life experiences can decrease anxiety. When students are provided information and proper support, they will have the tools to overcome any fears or anxiety and be able to experience, learn, and enjoy being outside!

Some teachers may initially resist implementing outdoor learning if they lack training, resources, and support. Pairing up teachers new to outdoor learning with more experienced teachers or having pairs of teachers work together to implement outdoor learning can help provide needed support. Providing training, time to meet and plan, and resources can help reluctant teachers get started with outdoor learning. If teaching outdoors is new and you find yourself alone in your desire to teach outside, don't be afraid to dive in and learn! In addition, the organization Inside-Outside, affiliated with Antioch University, has many chapters around the United States for teachers, school leaders, and others interested in outdoor learning. They also offer professional development and have many helpful resources on their website. You can find out more about them at insideoutside.org.

Materials for Outdoor Learning

There are a few materials that are utilized frequently in the activities and lessons in this book. Many of these materials you will already have in your classroom or available to you. Other materials needed for lessons will be found by the students in nature such as leaves, rocks, sticks, and pinecones. You may want to consider putting items such as sidewalk chalk on student supply lists at the beginning of the year. Also, don't forget that many classroom materials, such as math manipulatives, can also be used outside!

Suggested materials

- Sidewalk chalk
- Clipboards (dry erase boards, chalkboards, and sturdy pieces of cardboard can be converted to clipboards with binder clips) (see Figure 1.10)
- Permanent markers
- Field guides – plants, weeds, trees, animal tracks, birds, animals, etc. for your geographic area

Figure 1.10 Clipboards make an excellent surface for writing and drawing
Source: Andrew Chiappetta

Outdoor Learning Tip: Outdoor Notebooks

Having each student keep a devoted notebook for their outdoor work can help keep all the work done outdoors in one place. These notebooks are also a great place to do nature journaling. Children can write and draw their observations and record any questions they have. Beginning writers can simply draw (see Figure 1.11).

Figure 1.11 Students drawing observations of a bridge in their notebooks
Source: Andrew Chiappetta

Sturdy notebooks, preferably with a plastic cover, or composition notebooks with a rigid cardboard cover work best. For extremely wet and rainy areas, you may want to obtain notebooks designed for getting wet such as Rite in the Rain® notebooks. A sturdy canvas bag is a great way to keep all the notebooks together and can easily be grabbed on the way out the door. I suggest adding a stash of pencils and colored pencils in the bag too. Also, see the *Outdoor Learning Tip: Recording work in wet or snowy conditions* in chapter 3.

- Movable alphabet and numbers (plastic, wood, or letters painted on rocks used for spelling, math, writing, and games)
- Rubber bands
- Clipboards
- Measuring tapes or yard/meter sticks
- Scissors
- Clear tape

- Chart paper
- Containers for collecting such as empty peanut butter jars with tops, buckets
- Laminated cardstock for writing outside in wet weather
- Dry-erase colored pencils or crayons for writing outside in wet weather
- Plastic bag for trash or collecting natural items to examine more closely later

Additional lesson-specific materials

- Thermometer
- Bean bags (bought or DIY)
- Bird feeders and supplies
- Large 9 × 12 paper for class nature book
- Magnifying glasses

Final Thoughts

Now that you have picked a meeting area for your class, planned out your schedule, and talked with students and teachers about expectations and safety considerations, it is time to get your gear on and head outside! The next chapter will provide ideas to teach and reinforce reading, writing, and math skills in the schoolyard environment.

Note

1. M. Byron, C. Hron, A. Marturano, R. Pringle, J. Tesner Kleiner, and J. Wollum. "Positive Outdoor Experiences," Green Schoolyards America, https://www.greenschoolyards.org/positive-outdoor-experiences

02 Lessons in the Schoolyard

We begin by focusing on the schoolyard because it is the most accessible and convenient location to start implementing outdoor learning. Schoolyards and the area around the school can vary significantly in size, structure, and natural resources. A wide variety of activities are included to provide options for a range of outdoor settings. This chapter shows you how to utilize the space in your schoolyard for teaching lessons and reinforcing skills using chalk, natural materials, games, and playground equipment. Activities are organized into three categories: the wonders of chalk, using natural materials, and utilizing the schoolyard. Within each category, you will find activities broken up into sections for math, reading, and writing.

The Wonders of Chalk

Chalk is one of the best outdoor learning materials! It is affordable, and it can be used on artificial and natural surfaces and for a variety of activities. It is particularly useful for schools that have entirely paved outdoor spaces. In this section, you will find simple examples of activities that use chalk (see Figure 2.1). Many of these activities are based on similar activities you may already be doing inside the classroom, making them easy to integrate into preexisting lessons and curriculums. Using chalk outdoors for these activities can increase engagement and provide a multisensory element to the activities! If you plan to incorporate lots of chalk activities, you may wish to add sidewalk chalk and regular chalk (for finer detail and writing) to your school supply lists or ask if any parents would like to donate some to the class.

Math activities

Chalk is one of the easiest ways to bring math outdoors. It can transform nearly any problem, worksheet, or concept into a multisensory outdoor activity! In this section, you will find some familiar activities and math

Figure 2.1 Students using chalk in the schoolyard
Source: Angie Wright

strategies, such as ten frames and the lattice method of multiplication that can easily move outside. You will also find games and plenty of variations to meet the needs of students at different levels/grades.

Ten frames

Bring your ten-frame lessons and activities outdoors by making chalk ten frames and using natural materials as counters (see Figure 2.2).

Materials

- Draw ten frames with chalk or pieces of fabric with two ten frames drawn on it (with a permanent marker) for each student
- Natural materials such as rocks, acorns, or pinecones to use as counters (or bring your counters outdoors)
- Die or dice for the Roll to Twenty game

Activities

- **Model math facts:** Have students show math facts on a ten or twenty frame using two different natural materials and record the answers on paper or using chalk on the pavement.
- **Roll to Twenty:** Use two ten frames and a die for each pair of children to play the game Roll to Twenty. Players take turns rolling a die and

Outdoor Learning Tip: Chalk Cleanup Considerations

Some schools may have rules about where children can use chalk. Before planning activities using chalk, check with the administration about using chalk at your school and guidelines for cleanup. Some schools are more particular about chalk on the pavement and walls than others. If you need to clean walls or pavement after activities, provide students with spray bottles and water to wash away the chalk. Students love helping with this!

Figure 2.2 Chalk ten frame filled with flowers
Source: Rachel Tidd

placing the number of items indicated by the roll onto the ten frames. The first student to fill all twenty squares (or higher) wins the game. Play in reverse to practice subtraction.

- **Combinations:** Use chalk ten frames with two types of manipulatives to show all the possible combinations of ten or twenty.
- **Play collect 100:** Have children draw 10 ten frames and work together in groups to collect 100 natural items.
- **Skip counting:** Fill squares with multiple items or place value sticks for practicing skip counting (see Figure 2.3). (See the section on natural materials in this chapter to learn more about making place value sticks.)

Figure 2.3 Chalk ten frame filled with place value sticks to practice counting by tens
Source: Elizabeth Snyder

Adjusting this activity

For higher grades, try using chalk ten frames to practice repeated
addition, multiplication, or adding fractions.

Number lines

Number lines are a common strategy to model addition, subtraction, skip
counting, integers, and more inside the classroom. Number lines are a
great example of how the teaching methods you are likely already using
can easily be moved outdoors.

Materials

- Chalk
- Notebook
- Pencil
- Targeted numbers or math problems on cards or paper

Outdoor Learning Tip: Documenting Outdoor Work

If you have digital cameras, an iPad, or similar devices with cameras available in your classroom, students can use them to document work done outside with chalk or natural materials. This is an excellent way to keep a physical record of your students' work and the learning happening outdoors without having them copy everything onto paper.

Activity

Ask students to create a number line. You can specify the minimum, maximum, and intervals you would like the number line to have, or you may give the students the numbers they will need to place on the number line and have them construct it themselves.

Students should then place the numbers on the number line in the correct locations. You may wish to provide questions based on the finished number line for students to answer. For example, what is the number between 3 and 5? Which is larger, $\frac{2}{3}$ or $\frac{5}{6}$? Or what is $27 + 18$?

Variations

- **Skip counting:** Have groups or pairs of students draw a large number line and then practice skip counting by walking or jumping along the number line. Older students may practice skip counting with fractions or decimals such as $\frac{1}{2}$ or 0.25.
- **Fractions and decimals:** Try using outdoor number lines to place fractions, decimals, or a combination of both in order. This activity is great for building number sense with these more complex numbers!
- **Integers:** Introduce positive and negative numbers and have students practice adding and subtracting them.
- **Open number line:** Have students practice adding and subtracting multidigit numbers using an open number line. An open number line does not have a preset maximum, minimum, or interval. Instead, students write the first number of the problem on the line, then draw a series of "jumps" to add the second number. Usually, these jumps are in benchmark numbers, such as tens and ones (see Figure 2.4).

Figure 2.4 Using chalk to create an open number line
Source: Rachel Tidd

Number ladders

This activity is similar to word ladders, but the students use math operations to get to the next rung. These puzzles can be a great way to review skills and practice mental math skills outdoors!

Materials

• Chalk
• Pencil
• Paper
• Cards with numbers written or printed on them, such as 12 and 54

Activity

Divide students into pairs. Have them use chalk to draw a ladder with 6–8 rungs. Give them a card with two numbers. The first number listed is a starting number, and the second number is the ending number. Ask them to write the starting number on the top rung and the ending number on the bottom rung (see Figure 2.6). Their job is to move from the starting number to the ending number using mathematical operations. They can only perform one operation per step. Students record the operations next to each rung on the ladder and write the new number on the rung. When they are finished, they can switch with another group. The new group checks their work.

Outdoor Learning Tip: Alternative Number Line Methods

If you find yourself without a suitably paved area to draw a number line using chalk, try using a length of rope or a long stick for the line and either number rocks or leaves with numbers written on them to mark the intervals (see Figure 2.5). This is also a useful method if the schoolyard is covered in snow in the winter!

Figure 2.5 Using a stick for a number line
Source: Rachel Tidd

Adjusting this activity

- To make this activity easier, give students clues in the form of problems for each rung on the ladder (see Figure 2.6, 2.7). Depending on your students' needs, clues can vary from very basic to more complex.
- More advanced students can include fraction and decimal operations in their calculations.

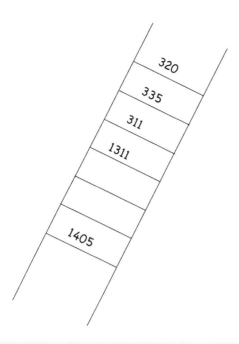

Figure 2.6 Example of a number ladder and the clues provided to the student

Clues:
1) 32 x 10
2) +15
3) –24
4) +1000
5) –20
6) +114
Final number=1405

Figure 2.7 Number ladder clues

Lattice multiplication

Students often prefer this method for solving multidigit multiplication problems. Why not take it outdoors?

Materials

- Sidewalk chalk
- Multiplication problems on cards or from a worksheet

Activity

Lattice multiplication can be practiced in all kinds of places when you use chalk! Sidewalks, walls, basketball courts, rocks, and more! Where will your students choose to do their multiplication work today? (See Figure 2.8.)

Give students cards or slips of paper with a few multiplication problems written on them and a piece of chalk. Then have them choose a location (or locations) to use the lattice method to solve their problems. Have them record their answers on the card or paper.

Adjusting this activity

Math problems of any type of strategy can be done outdoors. Using chalk to make number lines and traditional algorithms to solve math problems works well for any computation problem!

Figure 2.8 Lattice method for multiplication
Source: Rachel Tidd

Area method of multiplication

The area method of solving multidigit multiplication problems can be powerful for visual learners! It is also a strategy that students will be able to use all the way up to algebra! Using chalk to make large models of problems outdoors adds a new dimension to this strategy.

Materials

- Sidewalk chalk
- Multiplication problems

Activity

You may introduce the area method outside or simply have children practice using the area method outdoors using chalk. Use or provide different colors of chalk to show different sections.

Have children work in pairs or individually to solve a word problem that lends itself to the area method or simply give them a multidigit multiplication problem to solve (see Figure 2.9). Then have them "show and tell" how they solved the problem to another group.

Figure 2.9 Area method of multiplication
Source: Rachel Tidd

Reading and writing activities

Using chalk to practice phonics skills, word morphology, and spelling is a great way to get kids moving. Writing with chalk uses more muscle groups and provides more sensory feedback than writing with pencil and paper. It is often more appealing than paper-based writing activities in the class-room. Here are some activities to try with your class using chalk to practice reading and writing skills.

Word squares

Phonics squares are a great way for students to practice manipulating letters, graphemes, and spelling patterns, such as vowel teams, to create words.

Materials

- Sidewalk chalk
- Prepared cards with word squares for students to copy

Activity

Prepare small cards that show the word squares for children to copy the square onto the pavement using chalk. Giving groups different squares with phonics patterns selected based on students' needs can be a great way to differentiate and meet a wide range of reading levels.

Have children draw a 3 × 3 grid on a hard surface. Have them fill in the squares with the letters shown on the card (see Figure 2.10).

After they have recreated the word square, they can begin working together to find all the words that can be made using the letters.

r	b	l
m	ai	p
s	n	t

Figure 2.10 Example of a word square featuring the AI vowel team

When they discover a word, they should record the words in chalk next to the square or write them on paper.

How to make words using a word square:

To find words, start with one of the letters on the outside such as M, then slide over to AI, and then down to the letter N. What word does it make? MAIN! How many other AI words can they make from this square? They can move up, down, and diagonally (see Figure 2.10).

Adjusting this activity

Have older students work with prefixes and affixes. Ask groups to write the prefix or affix in the center box and then brainstorm or use a dictionary to find words that contain the prefix/affix in the surrounding boxes (see Figure 2.12). Have groups "solve" another group's square.

Figure 2.11 A student working on a word square
Source: Rachel Tidd

pack	wash	do	define
print	un-	re-	lock
tie	real	play	alarm

Figure 2.12 Example of a word square featuring prefixes

Word ladders

Word ladders are puzzles that help students practice segmenting and manipulating phonemes and graphemes to create words. Using chalk to bring this work outdoors, we transform a typical pencil-and-paper activity into one incorporating larger muscle groups and different writing textures.

Materials

- Sidewalk chalk
- Paper
- Pencil
- Cards with starting words and directions

Activity

Divide students into groups. Give each group a card with the starting word and directions for each new rung on their ladder (see Figure 2.13, 2.14). Have the students work together to figure out each word on the rung. They should write each answer on the rung. Then they apply the next clue to this word. This activity can be differentiated by giving groups different cards and directions.

Adjusting this activity

Word ladders are adaptable for many grade levels:

- Use CVC words and make the directions simple such as changing only one letter at a time.
- Select more complex words, affixes, prefixes, or verb forms and more complex directions for more advanced students.

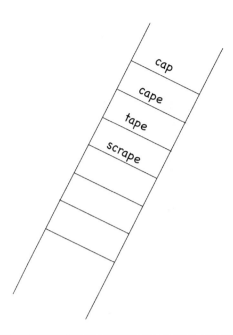

Figure 2.13 Example of a word ladder and clues provided to the student

Clues:
1) 3 letter word for hat.
2) A superhero wears a _ _ _ _.
(Add one letter)
3) Use this to fix a rip in a piece of paper. (Change one letter)
4) I have a _ _ _ _ _ _ on my knee.
(Change one letter and add two more)
5) The boy let out a _ _ _ _ _ _
as he went down the roller coaster.
(Change 3 letters)
6) The soccer _ _ _ _ cheered when they won the game. (Change one letter and take away 2 more)

Figure 2.14 Image of word ladder clues

Variation

Have students work in groups to design their word ladder. They can then write the directions on a card and exchange them with another group. Groups then draw a ladder and solve the puzzle designed by the other group!

There are many word ladder puzzles available online and in books such as the series *Daily Word Ladders* by Timothy Rasinski. These resources can be used to create more outdoor word ladders.

Word graffiti

Children love practicing spelling patterns, high-frequency words, phonics patterns, and vocabulary words when creating temporary chalk graffiti! This activity can be adapted for any grade level.

Materials

- Sidewalk chalk
- List of target words

Activity

Have children work individually or in pairs. Give them a list of words to practice by creating chalk graffiti (see Figure 2.15). After students have completed the activity, have the whole class tour everyone's new street art installations.

Adjusting this activity

Have older children write vocabulary words from other subjects or have them choose a new word from the dictionary. They could also make a symbol or picture to show the word's meaning. When students finish their work, go on a street art tour and visit each student's work. They can then share their word and the definition with the class. The youngest students can practice forming letters in the form of graffiti.

Extensions

- If your class is interested in street art and graffiti, many online lessons and resources can help you capitalize on this interest! Consider having students research the history of graffiti, debating the pros and cons, writing a persuasive essay outlining their argument for or against graffiti, etc.
- Look for street art in the neighborhood around your school or farther afield and take students on a walking tour/field trip to view the works. It can be fun to see how this influences their own art style! Look for murals, statues, tags, graffiti, and more (see Figure 2.16).

Figure 2.15 Students working on word graffiti in the schoolyard
Source: Rachel Tidd

- Lead a discussion about graffiti. Is it art? Should people be allowed to make graffiti? Does it add positively to the environment or does it detract?
- Use street art as a writing prompt. Students can write a story about the art or how the street art came to be there.

Learn more about street art and graffiti by sharing these books with your students:

- *Drawing on Walls: A Story of Keith Haring* by Matthew Burgess
- *Banksy Graffitied Walls and Wasn't Sorry* by Fausto Gilberti (recommended for upper grades as Banksy can be controversial)
- *Hey, Wall: A Story of Art and Community* by Susan Verde
- *Maybe Something Beautiful: How Art Transformed a Neighborhood* by F. Isabel Campoy and Theresa Howell

Figure 2.16 Murals and graffiti can inspire students' writing
Source: Rachel Tidd

Storyboards

Storyboards help students keep track of a story's main idea, plot, sequence, problem, solution, and more by having them illustrate the sequence of the story.

Storyboards allow children to visually break a story up into its main components. Storyboards can be made after read-alouds or following independent reading. In this version of storyboarding, children use natural materials and/or chalk to create their storyboards.

Materials

- Chalk
- Natural materials
- A story to summarize in a storyboard (this can be a story told orally, read out loud, or read independently)
- Optional: camera for taking pictures of the finished works

Activity

Depending on the age and preferences of your students, read, tell, or
have pairs of students write a story. Then have them use chalk to draw

rectangles that will form the "storyboard." Each rectangle represents a different part or event in the story. Students can use natural materials to create pictures representing each event and then use chalk to label each section. When finished, they can present their storyboard to the class. If you want permanent records of your students' work, I suggest taking photos of each group's work. Consider taking pictures of the entire board (or, if too large, several photos) and each panel. This will allow students to refer to the work in the classroom if you choose to extend the activity later.

Variations

- **History:** Try using storyboarding to break down historical events and periods.
- **Summarize:** Extend the activity by having students write a summary of the story using the storyboard for reference.
- **Story elements:** Instead of illustrating the events, have students use chalk/natural materials to show story elements.
- **Photo display:** Have students use the photos to create a display showing their work for a bulletin board or hall display. Adding a summary can add another element to the display as well. This can be a great way to show parents, other teachers, and even administrators how you integrate the outdoors into your classroom.
- **Natural materials:** Storyboard pictures can also be created using natural materials. For more permanent work or if created in an area without pavement, you can glue them on paper (see Figure 2.17).

Learning Games for the Schoolyard

Games always make learning more fun! Games are a great way to provide practice with math facts, high-frequency words, and spelling without worksheets. Taking games outside allows children to move more and be a bit louder than they can inside the classroom!

Math games

Math games are one of my favorite ways to get students to practice math facts, mental math, and other skills without worksheets or drills. Using

Figure 2.17 Illustrating story elements and the beginning, middle, and end with natural materials glued on to paper
Source: Rachel Tidd

stairs and jump ropes to practice skip counting gets kids moving. Games such as Scoot and snowball toss are fun, active alternatives to worksheets for skill practice.

Skip counting

Skip counting is more fun outside! Use jump ropes, stairs, and bean bags to add movement when learning this math skill! Skip counting can help reinforce multiplication facts in higher grades.

Materials

- Individual or longer group jump ropes
- Chalk
- Outdoor steps that you can write on with chalk
- Bean bags
- Various materials for variations

Skip Counting Rhymes

These are all rhymes children have sung jumping rope for generations! Children keep jumping when singing all these rhymes until they miss a jump. Substitute the counting with skip counting.

Blackbirds, Blackbirds

Blackbirds, blackbirds,
> Sitting on a wire.
> What do you do there?
> May we inquire?
> We just sit to see the day,
> Then we flock and fly away.
> By 1, 2, 3 . . . (insert any skip counting sequence here)

Cookies, Candies in a Dish

Cookies, candies in a dish.
> How many pieces do you wish?
> 1, 2, 3, 4 . . .

Hickety Pickety Pop

Hickety pickety pop,
> How many times before I stop?
> 1, 2, 3 . . .

Bubble Gum Bubble Gum

Bubble gum,
> Bubble gum,
> In a dish,
> How many pieces
> Do you wish?
> 1, 2, 3, 4, 5 . . .

How to play

Have children stand in a circle and pass the bean bag to the player on their right, saying the following number in the sequence. You can switch it up by changing how the bean bag is passed, making smaller groups, tossing it to students after saying their names, etc.

Variations

- **Stairsteps:** Have children use chalk to write each number in the skip counting sequence on the steps of an outdoor staircase. Then have them jump or step up, each one chanting the numbers to a rhythm.
- **Rhythm:** Have each student find two sticks and tap a rhythm while they chant (as a group) each number in the sequence.
- **Jump rope:** Practice skip counting by teaching children to jump rope. Jump roping combines large motor skills, coordination, rhythm, and skip counting in one activity. Jumping rope can be difficult for the youngest students. Model and teach students how to jump individually or with two people swinging the rope and one player jumping. Have them count to the rhythm of the rope hitting the ground. Many rhymes include counting. See the list of skip-counting rhymes in the sidebar. If you have children who are unable to jump, many of these rhymes can be chanted while tossing bean bags, clapping, or tapping to the rhythm.
- **Counting:** Prekindergarten through first grade students can use stairsteps, bean bags, and rhymes to practice counting forward and backward.

Bean bag toss

You can combine bean bags and chalk to create learning games! This version uses them to practice converting numbers into expanded form.

Materials

- 5–10 bean bags or stones (for each student)
- dice or cards with numbers written on them
- Chalk

Bean bags make a fun and easy activity for students to work on in class. They do not have to be perfect, just usable. If you are lucky enough to have a parent that likes to sew, this could be an excellent way for them to help! Bean bags can be used in all kinds of ways in the classroom, so having a class set can be a great resource.

If you do not have bean bags, rocks, pennies, or even some math manipulatives can be used. Test any potential material to ensure it does not roll or bounce too much. It can be frustrating during play!

How to play

The object of this game is to have students read a number and then break it into its components. For example, if the child drew a card with the number 326, they would need to convert it to expanded form: 300 + 20 + 6.

To set this game up, each group of students draws and labels a circle for each place value amount included in the game. For the preceding example, they would draw one circle for the hundreds, one circle for the tens, and one circle for the ones place. Then they decide on how far back they must stand to throw the bean bags from and draw a line. Players must be behind this line when it is their turn to throw.

When ready to play, the first player rolls three dice (or any number desired) or draws a number card. They then convert the number into expanded form.

They throw a bean bag at each place value spot equal to the number of hundreds, tens, or ones in their number. So, they get three shots at the hundreds because the number they drew has three one-hundreds. Then they get two tries at the tens and six attempts at the ones. They earn one point for each time their bean bag lands in the circle.

A few students in the group can return the bean bags or rocks to the player throwing. Others can keep track of points. The player with the most points after five rounds wins the game.

Playing with dice

Players roll the dice and make a three-digit number by arranging the dice. They can either make the largest number they can with the numbers they rolled OR roll each die one at a time. The first die is the hundreds place, the second die is the tens, and the final the ones. Use the number of dice appropriate for the number of digits you want in the game.

Variations

- Write numbers in the circle to have children to work on computation skills (see Figure 2.18). Players toss the bean bags into two different circles and add them together (or any desired operation). Students use estimation skills to aim for the largest numbers. The player with the largest total for each round gets one point. The student with the most points after five rounds wins.

Figure 2.18 Drawing circles for a variation of the bean bag toss game
Source: Jen Jensen

- Adjust the game to represent decimal place value. You can also change the points earned to contain decimal numbers to practice adding decimals.

Math fact toss-up

This can be a great whole group activity. Having students say each other's names aloud before throwing the ball helps keep everyone focused and engaged in the game!

Materials

- Large beachball or lightweight ball with multiplication (or other math facts) written on it
- Permanent marker

How to play

Have students stand in a circle. Students will toss the ball to each other. Before tossing the ball, they call out the name of the person they are tossing it to. After catching the ball, the student must answer the math fact that their right hand (or pointer finger if it is a smaller ball) lands on. After saying the answer, the student shouts another student's name and tosses the ball to them.

Variations

- **Elimination:** If students get the answer wrong, they sit down and are eliminated from the game. The last one standing wins.

- **Silent:** See if students can make sure everyone catches the ball and answers a problem without help or talking. They must pay close attention for this to work!
- **Dots and Shapes:** This game can be modified for the youngest students by drawing groups of dots on the ball to practice subitizing skills. (Subitizing is the ability to look at a group of objects and instantly know how many there are without counting them.)

Scoot

This is a great math game that can be used to practice any math skill! It can be done as a whole group or differentiated by breaking your class into two or three groups and giving different levels of problems or adjusting the time allowed before yelling "SCOOT!"

Materials

- Chalk for each student
- Paper with boxes numbered (for a large class, make a double-sided worksheet to ensure the boxes are big enough for calculations)
- Clipboards
- Pencils
- Timer

How to play

Line students up or arrange them in a large circular shape. Have them draw a large square on the pavement in front of them using chalk and then fill it with a math problem. You can give them parameters such as "fill the box with a multiplication problem" if you like or leave it up to the students! While they are writing, walk around and assign each student's square a number. The numbers should go in order. Have them write the number in the top left corner of their square. These numbers will help them know where to move next and where to record their answers. When they are finished writing the problems, it is time to play (see Figure 2.19).

Have students move to the square to their right (or the next number after their square) and set the timer. One or two minutes is usually perfect unless you have students doing more difficult problems. Have students begin solving the problem in the square right away! They can do calculations and write the answer in the box on their paper that matches the box number on the pavement.

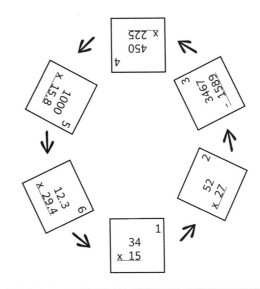

Figure 2.19 Example of scoot game setup

When the timer goes off, the teacher yells, "SCOOT!" Students take their paper and pencil and move to the next number. Keep playing until students have completed all the squares or time is up.

Variations

- You can premake cards with problems and arrange them on the ground. This allows you to have more control over the problems that the students solve. It also works well if you don't have a surface you can write on with chalk.
- Don't limit this game to math facts; try converting decimals to/from fractions, word problems, and measuring angles.
- You can also play this game with picture cards and have students write the word on their answer sheets.

Snowball target games

Harness students' love of snowball throwing and games with this activity. Snowball games are versatile and can be used to review or practice a range of academic skills!

Materials

- Packable snow
- Targets: bucket, bin, snow structure, etc.

- Area marked in the snow
- Labels to show points on the buckets or targets
- Set of cards with questions/problems that you would like students to practice for each group
- Laminated paper and writing utensil if problems require writing to find the answer (such as multidigit multiplication)

Activity

There are several ways you can approach this activity. For a teacher-directed approach, set up the bins or make targets and label them with points. Divide students into groups of four. Have students take turns drawing cards and answering the questions on the cards. If they get their question right, they can make and throw a snowball at the target. If they hit the target, they win the number of points indicated. Have students keep track of their points on laminated paper. You can use pictures drawn on the cards or targets for children not yet reading.

Variation

An alternative way to do this activity is for each group to develop a different version of a game using the materials provided (plus snowballs) to help them review the questions on the cards. Once they have come up with a game idea, they should play and test it out. To extend this version of the activity, have students record the game's rules so they can play again later, or groups can take turns teaching the class how to play their game and review different skills later.

Reading and writing games

Word games are a fantastic way for students to practice phonics, spelling patterns, high-frequency words, and grammar skills in a fun and engaging manner! Classic games such as hopscotch can be adjusted to practice a range of skills such as phonics patterns, high frequency words, and affixes. Games such as Change a Word give students hands-on practice with spelling, phonics, and phonological awareness.

Word tic-tac-toe

This is a fun variation on tic-tac-toe that is a great way to practice high-frequency and spelling patterns.

friend	friend	friend
said	friend	
said	said	

Figure 2.20 Example of word tic-tac-toe game

Materials

- Chalk
- Preselected words

How to play

Play just like regular tic-tac-toe, except instead of X's and O's, assign each player a high-frequency or spelling word they need to practice. They then write this word to mark their square (see Figure 2.20)!

Hopscotch

This classic game works great for practicing new phonics patterns, high-frequency words, and syllabication.

Materials

- Chalk
- Paved surface
- Rock or another object to be used as a marker

How to play

Hopscotch is typically played on a set of squares drawn in chalk on a paved surface. The most common pattern is a single square followed by two squares centered over the last square. This pattern repeats several times, creating the hopscotch path. Children often enjoy making creative hopscotch boards.

Once the board is complete, the first player throws a rock or other marker aiming for the first square. The player loses a turn if it lands on the line or outside the square.

The player then hops on the squares, skipping the square with the rock (see Figure 2.2). They hop on one foot when landing on single squares and put both feet down on double squares. They hop past their rock to the end and then hop back, picking up their rock at the end (stay on one foot!). Then skip over the square that held the rock and finish the path. If the player steps on a line or out of the square, they lose their turn. When finished, they pass the marker to the next player. The goal is to complete the course with the marker on each square. The first person to do this wins the game.

You can shorten the game for classroom play by limiting the number of rounds. To do this, decide on the number of rounds you would like the groups to play. Then have students label random squares with numbers up to the set limit. For example: If you wanted students to play four rounds, the students label four of the squares 1–4. The numbers can be written on any of the squares. Students begin play by throwing the rock on the square labeled with the number one.

Variations

- **Writing words with a phonics or spelling pattern or high-frequency word:** Follow the basic rules, but when a student throws a rock on the first square, they hop to the rock, write a high-frequency or spelling word, and then finish hopping back.
- **Reading high-frequency words:** Write high-frequency words in each square and have students read each word as they hop, skipping the square with the rock on it.
- **Sounds:** For beginning readers, write letters, digraphs, and blends on the squares and have them say the sounds as they hop.
- **Advanced options:** Fill in the squares with affixes, parts of speech, or literary devices (simile, metaphor, alliteration, personification, etc.). When they pick up the rock, they must give an example of a word or literary device indicated on the square.
- **Spell it out:** Write letters from a group of selected words on the squares. Have children draw a card with a picture of the word. They then must hop on the letters to spell the word without falling or going out of the lines!
- **Crazy boards:** Children often like to experiment with making the squares smaller (and therefore harder to hop on without falling or going over the line) or with new shapes and movements (spin, double-hop) (see Figure 2.22).

Figure 2.21 Playing hopscotch to review the digraph SH
Source: Rachel Tidd

- **Math:** Try playing the game using math facts. Write math facts on each square. Children have to say the answer to the fact where the rock lands.

Change a Letter game

The Change a Letter game is similar to word ladders; however, since it utilizes the movable alphabet, students can physically manipulate the letters to spell the word. This is a great way to work on manipulating phonemes, graphemes, phonics patterns, and spelling. To play, children switch out letters one step at a time, creating a whole chain of new words. They will see new connections and strengthen their ability to recognize parts of words as they play.

Materials

- Movable alphabet for each pair of students
- Cards or papers with directions for each round

Figure 2.22 A student's crazy hopscotch board
Source: Rachel Tidd

You will need to create directions for at least two different games. Divide students into pairs. Have one student read the directions and the other follow them. After the player solves the final clue, players switch roles and play the second game.

How to play

Directions for the Change a Letter game can range from simple (changing only one letter at a time) to changing more than one letter in more than one location (see Figure 2.23). Differentiate and adjust for different levels by modifying the difficulty of the directions and the words. See the following examples.

Example Directions (simple):

Use the movable letters and make the word RID. Then say, "Let's add one letter to make the word RIDE" (add the E at the end of RID). Keep going! Change the first letter to make the word HIDE. Keep going, following the directions below!

- Take away the H and add two letters to make SLIDE.
- Remove one letter to make SIDE.
- Change one letter to make WIDE.
- Change one letter to make WADE.
- Change one letter to make MADE.
- Change one letter to make MAKE.
- Change one letter to make BAKE.
- Take away one letter and add two letters to make SNAKE.

   Here is what you did: rid → ride → hide → slide → side → wide → wade → made → make → bake → snake

Example Directions (more complex):

Use your movable letters and make the word SPEAK.

- Change one letter and add one more to make STREAK.
- Take away one letter and change one letter to make SNEAK.
- Change two letters to make STEAM. (This is a bit more challenging because it requires changing the second and last letter.)
- Add one letter to make STREAM.
- Take away two letters and add one letter to make DREAM.
- Change one letter to make CREAM.
- Take away two letters and add one letter to make SEAM.
- Change one letter to make SEAT.
- Take away one letter and add two letters to make CHEAT.
- Take away two letters to make EAT.
- Add one letter to make EAST.
- Add one letter to make FEAST.
- Change one letter to make YEAST.

   Here is what you did: speak → streak → sneak → steam → stream → dream → cream → seam → seat → cheat → eat → east → feast → yeast

Figure 2.23 Playing the change a letter game
Source: Rachel Tidd

Variation

After playing one round each, have pairs of students write their own
series of directions. Then have them trade directions with another pair
of students and then both groups play using the new directions.

Playground words

Here is a quick and easy way to practice a variety of skills such as reading
words, sequencing, and vocabulary words by having students search the
playground for word cards.

Materials:

- Index cards or squares of paper
- Markers
- Tape

To differentiate groups or pairs of students' cards when searching for
them on the playground, write the words in different color markers OR
use different color index cards/paper for each group.

How to play

This activity is similar to a scavenger hunt. Prepare cards with words that
practice the target skill ahead of time (see variations below). Make a
set of cards for each group. Make sure the cards for each group are in

different colors. Have the students in each group hide a different group's cards around the playground and/or the schoolyard (see Figure 2.24).

Once all the cards are hidden, have each group find their cards. Depending on your goal for the activity, they may be copying the words, sorting the sounds, writing sentences or stories with the words, or defining vocabulary words.

Variations

- **Word reading:** Write target words or words with new phonics skills on cards for children to read and copy.
- **Vocabulary:** Write vocabulary words on cards and have students write the definitions or write the definitions and have the students come up with the vocabulary word.
- **Word sort:** Have the students sort words according to a phonics or spelling rule.
- **Sentences:** Use each word found in a sentence and record it.
- **Sequencing:** Put the sentences on the cards in sequential order to practice reading comprehension and sequencing skills.
- **Timeline:** Have students find historical events or events from a story and put them together in the form of a timeline.

Figure 2.24 An older student hiding words on the playground for a younger class
Source: Rachel Tidd

- **Riddles:** Read and guess the riddles.
- **Parts of speech:** Sort words into nouns, verbs, and adjectives.
- **Scrambled words:** Write letters or words on the cards and have students unscramble and find the message.
- **Try other locations:** This scavenger hunt can be done in almost any location, parks, neighborhood, woods, and cemeteries.

Sentence challenge

This simple game can be adapted for use in many grades and skills! You can use it to reinforce punctuation skills, semantics, spelling, homophones, and more.

Materials

- Chalk for each student or pair of students

How to play

Divide students into groups. Give or tell them various components of a sentence, all mixed up. Groups need to reconstruct the sentence and record it with chalk on the pavement. The first team to raise their hand reads their sentence aloud. If it is correct, they get the point. If it is incorrect, the next fastest team receives a chance to win the point. The team with the most points wins.

Variations

- **Punctuation matters:** Read or say a sentence, have students write it, and include punctuation that matches the tone or way you said it.
- **Homophones:** Announce a homophone. Students need to write a sentence showing the different meanings of the word and spell them correctly! (See Figure 2.25.)
- **Parts of a sentence:** Give a verb, adjective, and noun and have students construct a creative sentence using the words.
- **High-frequency word sentences:** Have the youngest students write a sentence using a high-frequency word.
- **Spelling word sentences:** Have pairs of students take turns writing sentences using spelling words or a targeted phonics pattern. For an extra challenge, have them make the sentences tell a story!

Figure 2.25 Writing sentences using the homophones *know* and *no*
Source: Rachel Tidd

Using Natural Materials

Children cannot resist natural materials such as pinecones, shells, acorns, and small rocks! Using natural materials as manipulatives in your lessons increases student engagement. The best part is that natural material manipulatives are readily available, can be used indoors or out, and are usually free! In this section, you will find simple ways to use natural materials as manipulatives in your lessons (see Figure 2.26). You can also perform many of these activities in locations farther afield.

Depending on where your school is located, you may collect natural materials right in your schoolyard, in nearby parks, the neighborhood (nuts, seeds, leaves, and sticks often fall onto the sidewalk), or even plan a short trip farther afield to gather materials. Children love to help collect natural learning materials. Assign groups to collect materials such as sticks, pinecones, small rocks, etc. Use materials that are found or grow locally and are plentiful. You can also enlist help from students' families to collect items for both the indoor and outdoor classroom and have them send them to school. Storing the collected materials in clear containers or baskets makes them accessible and visually appealing. You may find that children

Figure 2.26 Children counting and grouping horse chestnuts
Source: Remona St. John

prefer using natural materials (especially if they helped gather them) over traditional plastic manipulatives. Common natural materials for use as manipulatives are:

- Small rocks
- Leaves
- Pinecones
- Acorns, chestnuts, butternuts, sweetgum, walnut shells
- Maple seed "helicopters"
- Seashells
- Sticks (see place value sticks in the math section)
- Flowers or petals (use common flowers such as dandelion)
- Tree cookies (slices of a branch cut with a saw)
- Clover blossoms or clover leaves
- Pine needles

General activities

Students can use rocks and leaves with numbers and letters written on them to practice math, reading, and writing skills in a variety of ways! This section provides guidance for making your own set of letter and number rocks and ideas for using them. Activities such as leaf flower sorts to practice math and phonics skills make learning hands-on and fun.

Outdoor Learning Tip: Leaf Sorts, Matching, and Memory Games

Leaves can be used just as you would index cards or small pieces of paper. Consider using them for word sorts, matching activities, sentence building, and games such as memory. Permanent markers write perfectly on the leaf's surface. If leaves are out of season or difficult to find, you can use index cards outside (see Figure 2.27).

Figure 2.27 Words written on leaves for creating silly sentences
Source: Rachel Tidd

Letter and number rocks

Students learning to read can get hands-on practice reading and manipulating words by using a set of letters (see Figure 2.28). Montessori schools use a movable alphabet, which is a set of letters A–Z. Each letter has multiple copies, and the consonants and vowels are typically different colors. Using movable letters helps target reading or spelling skills without layering on writing skills. This method benefits all students but can be particularly helpful for children with dyslexia or dysgraphia.

Figure 2.28 Practicing high-frequency words with letter rocks
Source: Rachel Tidd

Using sets of letters outdoors to write, read, and practice spelling works extremely well on a variety of surfaces and weather conditions. Many teachers use plastic or wooden letters in a similar way inside their classrooms.

Movable alphabets do not have to be made of natural materials. They can also be constructed from plastic magnetic letters, wooden letters, letters written on wooden disks, or other creative solutions! Plastic containers for crafting typically have many compartments and work well to keep letters organized and are easily taken outdoors.

Creating a few sets of movable alphabets for your classroom is relatively simple. Rocks are a great choice as they are easy to gather or purchase. For this project, rocks with a smoother surface are best, as you will need to write letters and numbers on them. If you have trouble finding suitable rocks, the floral department of craft stores or even the dollar store sells bags of rocks suitable for this project.

Once you have your rocks, simply write the letters on the rocks. Make several copies of each letter, especially the vowels. It can be helpful to make the vowels and consonants different colors. Typically, vowels are red, and consonants are blue (if your rocks are very dark, consider pastel colors).

If using paint markers on smooth-textured rocks, a coat or two of Mod Podge can help make them more durable.

Consider making rock sets with the numbers 1–10 including the symbols for computation (+, −, ×, ÷) to use in outdoor math lessons. You can make rocks with dots for younger students to practice subitizing skills. In the winter, you can use letter and number silicone molds filled with colored water to make ice letters and numbers! These are fun to use in the snow!

Materials:

- Rocks or tree cookies
- Two colors of permanent markers or paint markers (typically red and blue)

Optional materials

- Paint
- Mod podge™ (can help protect the paint from chipping off)
- Various materials for specific activities

Activities using letter rocks

- **Letter sound hunt:** Have young children find items that begin or end with a selected sound or letter.
- **Handwriting:** Have young children use the letters as models for writing letters with chalk.
- **Sound or Elkonin boxes:** Use the letters in sound boxes (Elkonin) drawn with chalk or in the snow/dirt with a stick.
- **Marking up words:** Show the component parts of words by labeling words written with the movable alphabet to show vowel sounds, digraphs, vowel teams, syllables, and more (see Figure 2.29).
- **Change a Letter game:** Play the Change a Letter game (see the Games section in this chapter).
- **Spelling:** Practice spelling words or new phonics patterns. Dictate words and have children or groups spell them using the letters. This activity can be adjusted for any age!
- **Crossword game:** Play a version of Scrabble® outside by having players take turns to build words that connect like a crossword puzzle.
- **Picture card spelling:** Have children spell words shown on picture cards or identify the beginning, end, or middle sounds.
- **Learn and label plant species:** Have students gather flowers, leaves, and plant specimens and lay them on a flat outdoor surface. Use the

Figure 2.29 Labeling or "marking up" words to show their vowel
sounds and other features
Source: Rachel Tidd

rock letters to label each species. Have older students include the
Latin names.

- **Word scramble:** Give groups one large word and have them use the
letters in the word to create as many words as possible and record
them. The group with the most real words wins! For example, you give
the word **sunshine** to the class. Each group selects the letters from the
movable alphabet to spell **sunshine**. Then they move and rearrange
the letters from the word sunshine to create new words such as hen,
shin, and shines.
- **Silly sentences:** Use the letters for children to write silly sentences.
- **High-frequency word practice:** Practice writing sight or high-
frequency words.

Activities using number rocks

- **Number sentences:** Show a model of a problem and use the numbers
to write a number sentence.
- **Order of Operations:** Have students write equations to practice the
order of operations and how the placement of parenthesis can change
the answer. For example, students could write and solve $(3 + 8) \times 9 =$
_____ And $3 + (8 \times 9) =$ ____ (see Figure 2.30).

Figure 2.30 Using number rocks to practice order of operation
problem – sticks are used as parentheses
Source: Rachel Tidd

- **Time:** Have students build a clock using number rocks and sticks as hands to practice reading and showing different times (see Figure 2.31).
- **Reduce writing demands:** Use number rocks to practice math facts without the added handwriting component.
- **Fact families:** Practice and record fact families (addition/subtraction, multiplication/division) such as 2 + 3 = 5, 3 + 2 = 5, 5 − 2 = 3, and 5 − 3 = 2.
- **Record answers:** Use the number rocks to record answers from a worksheet or word problem instead of writing.

Leaf flower sorts

Leaf flower sorts use leaves as petals to create flowers for each attribute or category being sorted. They are incredibly versatile and can be used to sort phonics patterns, fact families, root words or suffixes, character traits, science concepts, and more!

Materials

- Rocks for the center of the flower (you can also use paper circles or branch slices)
- Leaves for petals

Figure 2.31 Using number rocks to create a clock and practice telling time
Source: Rachel Tidd

- Chalk
- Permanent marker
- Prepped list of words or leaves with prewritten words, facts, or other selections to be sorted
- Paper and pencil

Activity

This activity works best when you write the words (or whatever category you are having students sort) on the leaves using a permanent marker ahead of time. More advanced students can be given a list and then can write the words or selections on the leaves.

Divide students into pairs and ask them to label each rock with a category. Then, give students prepared leaves or a list of words/items to copy onto leaves with a permanent marker. Then have students sort the leaves, placing the stem of the leaf under the rock whose category the word or selection matches. As leaves are added to each rock, it creates a beautiful flower (see Figure 2.32)! You may wish to have students record each category and the words or selections on paper after sorting.

Variations

- **Silly sentences:** Write words on leaves for children to arrange into silly sentences. Have them record each sentence in their notebooks.
- **Leaf paper:** Leaves can be used to practice writing sentences, making flashcards, and more!
- **Color sorts:** Preschool and kindergarten students can sort leaves by color or create a color gradient.

Math with natural materials

Figure 2.32 Using leaves to sort addition fact families
Source: Rachel Tidd

Using natural materials is a great way to integrate nature into your math lessons. Children often are attracted to natural materials and find them more pleasing than typical plastic math manipulatives. We can capitalize on this interest by using these materials in our math lessons.

Place value sticks

Place value sticks are bundles of ten sticks used in place of base ten blocks to teach math skills involving place value or skip counting. This activity enlists the help of students in creating a classroom set of place value sticks that can be used to practice place value indoors and outdoors. Making place value sticks is as much a part of the learning process as using them.

Materials

- At least 120 small sticks collected by students or gathered by the teacher beforehand
- Rubber bands
- Pencil (or chalk)
- Paper
- Large bin or basket for storing the completed stick bundles

Activity

Involving students in creating a class set of place value sticks allows children to apply their math skills to solve a problem. Ask each group to collect 120 small sticks. Alternatively, divide the total number of sticks desired by the number of groups. Each stick should be approximately six inches long and about the circumference of a pencil. Make sure to emphasize that sticks should be on the ground, not taken off live trees.

Have the groups discuss and decide how they will collect and keep track of the number of sticks they have, how many they still need, and a plan to keep them all organized! The real magic of this activity is when children are actively keeping track of how many sticks they have collected. Each time they add more sticks they must recalculate! Provide chalk or pencil and paper for any calculations they might want to make. Omit this if you would like to encourage mental math.

Once the groups have the correct number of sticks, tell them that you need ten bundles of ten sticks and 20 single sticks and distribute the rubber bands. The rubber bands are used to bundle the groups of ten sticks together.

Now that you have a class set of place value sticks, use them as you would using typical base ten blocks. Use them to represent larger numbers in tens and ones, show how to regroup multidigit addition or subtraction problems, and skip count by having the students re-bundle the sticks into groups of a different quantity (see Figures 2.33 and 2.34).

Outdoor Learning Tip: More Ways to Use Natural Materials

Natural materials can be used in so many ways that it is impossible to cover them all here. You can substitute natural materials in almost any lesson that uses typical manipulatives.

Additional ways to use natural materials

- **Subitizing:** Use materials in subitizing activities. For example, show students subitizing dot cards for a few seconds and have them re-create the arrangement with the natural materials (see Figure 2.35).
- **Number bonds:** Sticks and number rocks can be used to model number bonds (see Figure 2.36).
- **Odd and even:** Use natural materials to make a model to determine if a number is odd or even.
- **Model Multiplication:** Model multiplication as equal groups using natural materials.

Figure 2.33 Using place value sticks to add
Source: Rachel Tidd

Figure 2.34 Using place value to practice regrouping in multi-digit addition problems
Source: Rachel Tidd

Figure 2.35 A student practices subitizing using natural materials to re-create a dot pattern after being shown the pattern on a card for a few seconds
Source: Rachel Tidd

Figure 2.36 Using number rocks and sticks to model
number bonds
Source: Rachel Tidd

Stick geometry

Pavement, sidewalks, and snow make excellent surfaces for using sticks to construct shapes. This activity is a fun way to learn about shapes and their attributes in a hands-on way. This activity can be adapted for the upper grades by having students calculate the perimeter and area of each shape created.

Materials

- Enough sticks for each pair of students
- Ruler
- Laminated paper and dry-erase writing utensil for recording

Preparation

If your schoolyard does not have many sticks or you do not already have a collection of suitable sticks, you may need to collect sticks in a park or natural area for this activity. If you have a good supply of sticks on school grounds, you may wish to have students collect them before-hand. Make sure to emphasize that sticks should be on the ground, not taken off live trees.

After introducing shapes and their attributes such as corners, sides, and
    angles, divide students into pairs. Each pair of students should have
    enough sticks to construct each shape and extra sticks to create a
    new shape.

Ask students to make a shape with the fewest number of sticks. What is
    the only shape they can make? (Triangle.) Have them record the num-
    ber of sides and corners using a three-column chart on their lami-
    nated paper. Older students can also calculate and record the perime-
    ter and area of the shape.

What kinds of shapes can they make with four sticks? Have them record
    the attributes of the new shape on their chart. Discuss their findings.

Continue the activity by adding more sticks. Which number makes the
    largest variety of different shapes?

Have students create a shape larger than the shapes they previously
    made. Have them record the attributes and name the shape (if it is a
    new shape, have them create a name that is more descriptive than the
    term polygon!).

Variation

A similar activity can be done using sticks to model and measure angles.
    For this activity, students need a protractor.

Creating arrays

Arrays are an excellent way for students to model multiplication and find
the factors of numbers. Using natural materials readily available outside
can allow children to practice modeling multiplication problems and help
them solve them. In the lower grades, children can use arrays for counting
items arranged in a line, rectangular array, or counting rows and columns.

Materials

- Natural materials (or snowballs)
- Notebook or laminated paper for recording
- Pencils or dry-erase pencils

Activity

Model how to construct arrays for a number using natural materials or
    snowballs (in winter) (see Figure 2.37). Then have students work indi-
    vidually or in pairs to find all the possible arrays for a given number.

Outdoor Learning Tip: Using Snow to Make Arrays

While these activities focus on creating arrays using natural materials such as rocks and pinecones, snow can also be an excellent medium for making arrays. Children can make snowballs to model multiplication arrays or draw grids in the snow.

Figure 2.37 Modeling arrays using rocks
Source: Rachel Tidd

They should record all the combinations and write the factors/multiplication facts for each number. Ask a few students to share their work with the class (the physical arrays they made and the recorded notes).

Adjusting the Activity

Students working on counting can build and count objects in ten frames or larger arrays. They can also count rows or columns in an array.

Modeling fractions with natural materials

Using natural materials to model fractions gives children lots of hands-on experience creating, interpreting, and manipulating fractions.

Materials

- Circle, square, and rectangle cake pans
- Sand, mud, or snow
- Stick or plastic knives
- Natural materials

Sourcing cake pans

Collect old cake pans from parents, thrift stores, and garage sales, or purchase aluminum or inexpensive pans at the dollar store.

Activity

Using natural materials to model fractions is the simplest way to take
fraction work outside. Use objects to model ¼ by showing one acorn
and three pinecones. The acorn is ¼ of the collection.

Variation

Have students use scissors and cut leaves to show the fractions ½ and ¼
and lines of symmetry.

Modeling fractions with mud pies

Mud pies are a fun and engaging way to teach fractions outdoors! Prefill
the pans with mud, sand, or snow, depending on what you have available,
and the season.

Materials

- Circle, square, and rectangle cake pans
- Sand, mud, or snow
- Stick or plastic knives
- Natural materials

Activity

Model for students how to show different fractions on a mud pie by
using a stick or plastic knife to "cut" the cake into fractional parts. Use
natural materials to highlight other fractional parts (see Figure 2.38).
For example, use blades of grass to cover two of the three cake pieces
to show the fraction ⅔.

Then have children make and decorate their cakes using natural materials
in fractional sections of their choice. Ask them to record their decora-
tions and the fractional part of the cake each decoration covers. These
will serve as directions for another cake decorator (student). Can a

Figure 2.38 Example of using mud pies to model fractions
Source: Rachel Tidd

friend re-create their cake from their directions? When finished, they can also share their designs with others or the whole group.

Modeling equivalent fractions with mud pies

You can also use cake pans to model fraction operations (see Figure 2.39)! So often students memorize how to solve fraction problems without really understanding what the steps they are performing mean. By providing plenty of opportunities to experiment with solving these types of problems using cake pan models, students will gain an in-depth understanding of fraction operations.

Materials

- Circle, square, and rectangle cake pans
- Sand, mud, or snow
- Stick or plastic knives
- Natural materials

Activity

Here is an example of how to model finding equivalent fractions with mud pies using cake pans. Have students begin by drawing three

Figure 2.39 Using mud pies to model finding equivalent fractions
Source: Rachel Tidd

vertical lines on the cake (this will create fourths). Have them use natural materials such as grass or pine needles to mark three of the four parts. This will show the fraction ¾ (see Figure 2.40).

Next, have them use a stick to make a horizontal line through the middle of the pan. Ask, "What size are the pieces of cake now?" The cake is now divided into eighths (see Figure 2.41). Ask, "Our original fraction was ¾. How can we describe the same fractional part of our cake in eighths?"

The fractional part of the cake did not change. Both ¾ and ⁶⁄₈ describe the same amount of cake. We call these equivalent fractions. Have them write these two fractions on paper or with number rocks or plastic numbers.

Ask your students if they see any patterns or ways in which the two equivalent fractions they wrote are related (you can see this in numerical representations I wrote under each square).

A conversation with your students might sound like this: "We can multiply the denominator by two to get eighths in our equivalent fraction. Does multiplying the numerator by two give us the correct number? Yes! To get an equivalent fraction, we multiplied the numerator and denominator by the same number. Does this rule work for finding other equivalent fractions in our other squares?"

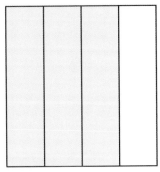

Cake pan showing 3/4.

Figure 2.40 Cake pan showing the fraction 3/4

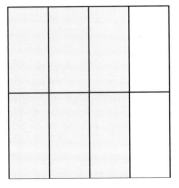

**Figure 2.41 Cake pan with a stick laid across to make eighths –
the fraction is now 6/8: $\dfrac{3 \times 2 = 6}{4 \times 2 = 8}$**

Next, have them record a drawing of the fractions made in the pan and the equation in their notebook. Then, have them do the same process again. This time they will add another horizontal line to create twelfths (see Figure 2.42).

Variations

You can use cake pan models to add, subtract, multiply, and divide fractions.

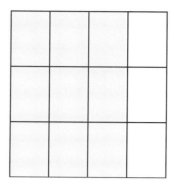

Figure 2.42 Cake pan with two sticks laid across to make twelfths – the fraction is now 9/12: $\dfrac{3\times3}{4\times3}=\dfrac{9}{12}$

3D shapes in the snow

Snow makes a fantastic modeling material for creating and learning about 3D shapes and volume. This hands-on activity utilizes recycled and re-purposed containers to create shapes and identify their attributes and the type of shape. Older students can calculate the shape's volume.

Materials

- Snow (wet sand or kinetic sand can also be used if snow is not available)
- Recycled or repurposed containers in various geometric shapes
- Ruler
- Laminated paper
- Dry-erase colored pencils or crayons

Activity

Divide students into pairs or groups and provide each group with several containers. Model how to pack the containers with snow and flip them over, resulting in a 3D shape. Explain the attributes and metrics you would like them to record for each shape created: number of sides, corners, length of sides, area of sides, shape name if known, shapes of sides, and total volume. The metrics you choose will vary depending on the age/grade of your class.

Have older students calculate the surface area and volume of the shapes.

Have students combine all the containers and sort them according to different attributes such as the shapes of the sides, the total number of corners, and if they contain a rounded edge or their general size.

Reading and writing activities using natural materials

Natural materials can also enhance lessons in reading comprehension and writing skills. Leaves are especially useful for modeling and practicing contractions, prefixes, and suffixes. Children love using natural materials such as clay to create a character and using leaves and other materials to make masks for acting out a story.

Masks and playacting

Students love acting out stories whether they are from a book or stories they have written themselves. Adding masks constructed from natural elements adds to the fun! This activity also works well for pairing older student mentors with younger students.

- Cardboard or cardstock
- Scissors
- Glue
- Tape
- Various natural materials (collect the materials ahead of time as a separate activity if you only have a paved area at your school or have children find their own as part of the activity if your schoolyard has sufficient materials available)
- Paper and pencil if students are writing their script or familiar picture books if children are acting out the stories from books

Divide students into groups and have them create a skit. They should work together to write the script, choose parts, and practice performing. You may give them a topic or theme (based on an animal or plant they recently saw, a current topic of study, or choose to let them freely create. Once they have written the script, they can make masks for the characters using cardboard, string, and glue or tape (see Figure 2.43).

Activity: Reading comprehension emphasis

Students can do a similar activity using familiar picture books. Have students work in groups to practice acting out the story of a familiar picture book. Children can read the text or retell the story in their own words, using the pictures for reference. While the "narrator" is reading or telling the story, the other children act it out. Have them create masks for each character to use as a costume. They can use cardboard, string, glue or tape, and natural materials to create the masks. Groups will need to practice their performance a few times. When they are ready, ask groups to take turns performing for the whole group!

Figure 2.43 Acting out a story wearing a mask made from natural materials
Source: Rachel Tidd

Leaf syllables

Learning to segment syllables is a vital skill for children as they learn to read. It builds phonological awareness, helps with decoding words, and supports spelling skills. Using leaves to cut words to show where each syllable divide is located is an excellent hands-on way to practice this skill outdoors. If you do not have leaves in your schoolyard, gather them in parks, sidewalks, or other public greenspaces. This activity is best after a lesson on dividing words with a specific syllable pattern such as words with a VCCV (vowel-consonant-consonant-vowel) pattern.

Materials

- Leaves
- Permanent markers
- Glue
- Paper

Activity

Give each child or pair a list of words to divide into syllables. This can be on a piece of paper or written on a chalkboard or dry-erase board for the whole class to see. Children copy each word onto the leaves. Next, they choose one leaf and decide where to divide the syllables. Then they can cut the leaf in the selected spot using scissors (see Figure 2.44). They should then lay each word part side by side, leaving a small space between them to visually show how the word is divided into syllables. If desired, have children copy the words, noting the syllable divisions, onto paper or glue the leaf parts onto paper.

Leaf contractions

Children often need lots of practice when learning how to combine words into a contraction. Leaves are readily available and make the perfect material to model and practice concepts. Modeling contractions using leaves provides a multisensory way to practice this skill.

Materials

- Minimum of 10 leaves per child/pair
- Permanent markers

Figure 2.44 Dividing syllables in words written on leaves
Source: Rachel Tidd

- Small natural materials for apostrophes such as a small stick, blade of grass, etc.

- Chalk or pencil/paper for recording the final contractions

Activity

For this activity, you will need at least 10 leaves per child. Leaves with a long, thin shape from the same plant or tree work best.

Provide the child or small group with a list of five word pairs that can be combined to make contractions. Have them copy each word onto a leaf. When they are ready to make a contraction, they look at the two words in a pair and decide which letters to snip off. Then they push the remaining parts of the words together and form the contraction. Use a small stick or other natural material as an apostrophe. When they have finished constructing all the contractions, they may copy them onto paper or on a hard outdoor surface using chalk (see Figure 2.45).

Figure 2.45 Cutting words written on leaves to create contractions
Source: Rachel Tidd

Leafixes (prefixes and suffixes with leaves)

Using leaves to model adding prefixes and suffixes to root words is another excellent way to utilize leaves. For this activity, students overlap leaves with the suffixes and prefixes on top of the leaf with the root word to form new words. This activity can be an excellent follow-up to a spelling or vocabulary lesson.

Materials

- Leaves
- Permanent markers
- Paper or notebook
- Pencil

Activity

Provide children with a list of root words and prefixes/suffixes. Have them write the root words, prefixes, and suffixes on leaves. Have them experiment with adding the suffixes and prefixes in different combinations to the root words. How many real words can they create? Ask students to record all the (real) words that they create!

Clay characters

Creating a brand-new creature using clay and natural materials makes for an engaging way to teach character development, character traits, and writing skills.

Materials

- Clay (or homemade playdough)
- Natural materials
- Pencil
- Paper

Activity

Give each student a ball of clay and access to natural materials such as sticks, leaves, rocks, bark, and mulch. Ask students to use the clay and materials to create a new character. When finished have students write about their character.

- What is their name?
- What is their personality?
- Where are they from?
- Where do they live?
- What are some of their character traits?

Then they can write a short story featuring the character they developed. Students should try to incorporate at least one of the character's traits in the story. Alternatively, you may have students act out their stories with their clay characters to practice oral language skills.

Utilizing the Schoolyard

Schoolyards and playgrounds are not just for recess! They can be excellent locations to demonstrate science concepts and practice design skills! This section shows you how to capitalize on the resources in your schoolyard and provides a few suggestions on items to enhance learning!

Math and science activities

This section contains activities that utilize the schoolyard space to learn math or science concepts. Several of the activities incorporate both math and science skills together in one activity, such as learning about birds and collecting data about them.

Outdoor Learning Tip: Recording Work in Wet or Snowy Conditions

Using paper to record work in wet or snowy conditions can be difficult. One simple solution is to make a class set of laminated cardstock. When laminated, the paper is waterproof and can be used as a writing surface with a dry-erase marker. If temperatures are below freezing, dry-erase markers may not work. If you experience very cold temperatures often, try dry-erase crayons or colored pencils.

Attracting birds

Watching birds provides endless learning opportunities. Observing and learning about bird behavior, different species, migration patterns, and changes in plumage in different seasons are just some of the topics children can learn from a simple bird feeder. Using bird observation as the basis for graphing and data collection is another way to utilize a schoolyard bird feeder!

NOTE You may need permission to add a bird feeder to your window and/or schoolyard.

Materials

- Bird feeder
- Bird seed
- Bird guides

Setting up Your Feeder

You can ask local hardware or home supply stores if they are willing to donate feeders and feed. Parents may also be willing to donate seeds or an unused bird feeder to lend or donate.

There are many different styles of bird feeders. Some can be attached to a window; some are designed to hang from a tree or pole. Bird feeders also are designed for different types of birds: small birds such as chickadees, larger birds such as cardinals, and suet feeders for cardinals. Choose a bird feeder to attract the types of birds most common in your geographical area. If the feeder will be close to the building and/or over a paved surface, plan to sweep up the empty seed shells periodically.

If possible, choose a location for the feeder that you can see from the classroom windows. This allows you to observe birds both outside and inside! If this is not possible, choose somewhere away from busy areas like the playground. If the feeder is not visible from your classroom, plan to visit regularly. You can have children write down observations in their nature journals.

Activity suggestions

- **Track species:** Track all the different species that visit your feeders over time. Make a list on chart paper and hang it somewhere accessible to the children so they can add new species independently!
- **Track the number of birds:** Observe and track the number of birds of each species that visit the feeder. Use the data to construct graphs.
- **Bird behavior:** Observe and discuss bird behavior. How do smaller birds act when larger birds fly in? Do they ever fight? How do they communicate? Does their behavior change with the weather or seasons?
- **Learn bird identification:** Learn to identify birds using characteristics such as size and shape, color pattern, behavior, and habitat. Learn more and watch free videos at https://www.allaboutbirds.org/news/building-skills-the-4-keys-to-bird-identification/
- **Research a species:** Have students research a bird species and write a report. This can be done in groups, with each group sharing with the class what they learned.
- **Citizen science project:** Participate in a citizen science project. The Cornell Lab of Ornithology hosts several citizen science projects such as the Great Backyard Bird Hunt. These projects have students collect and submit data about the number and species of birds observed during specific periods. This can be an excellent way for children to participate in real science research! They have a packet of resources, including an excellent bird species poster associated with Project FeederWatch, as well as many free classroom lesson ideas about birds! Some excellent resources for citizen science projects related to birds are: Project FeederWatch at feederwatch.org, Backyard Bird Count found at birdcount.org, Cornell University's K–12 Resources found at birds.cornell.edu/k12/, and Urban Birds at celebrateurbanbirds.org.

Suggested Books About Birds

A well-stocked classroom library can inspire and feed your young birders' curiosity! Here are some favorites!

- *Beaks!* by Sneed B. Collard III
- *Whose Beak Is This?* by Gillian Candler
- *The Big Book of Birds* by Yuval Zommer
- *Our Yard Is Full of Birds* by Anne Rockwell
- *The Sibley Guide to Birds* by David Allen Sibley
- *Unbeatable Beaks* by Stephen Swinburne
- *Woodpecker Wham!* by April Pulley Sayre
- *Ruby's Birds* by Mya Thompson
- *Bird Count* by Susan Edwards Richmond (this pairs well with citizen science bird count activities)
- *Brave Wolf and the Thunderbird* by Joe Medicine Crow
- *Have You Heard the Nesting Bird?* by Rita Gray
- *Animals in Flight* by Robin Page
- *Flute's Journey: The Story of a Wood Thrush* (short chapter book) by Lynne Cherry
- *An Eagle's Feather* by Minfong Ho
- *All the Birds in the World* by David Opie
- *Feathers Not Just for Flying* by Melissa Stewart
- *The Real Poop on Pigeons!* by Kevin McCloskey
- *The Boy Who Drew Birds: A Story of John James Audubon* by Jacqueline Davies
- *Crow Smarts: Inside the Brain of the World's Brightest Bird* by Pamela Turner

Design a playground

What would your students do if they could completely redesign the playground? This STEM activity has students redesign their school playground.

Materials

- Pencil
- Large pieces of paper
- Access to the playground or area that students wish there was a playground

Optional

- Recycled or found materials or blocks for building a model
- Glue
- Tape

Add a Weather Station to Your Schoolyard

Children of all ages love to observe the weather! Small-scale weather stations take a little setup and some can be mounted outside the classroom window. The most basic type measures indoor and outdoor temperature and humidity and tracks the lowest and highest temperature recorded. More advanced weather stations also track atmospheric pressure, rain accumulation, and wind speed.

They are a simple way to take advantage of the schoolyard and encourage children to connect with the natural world. Some schools have children report the weather from the weather station during morning announcements. See chapter 5 for ideas on how to integrate weather observation into your morning meeting.

Activity

Lead a discussion with students about the playground (if you do not have one, imagine one!). What would they change or add if given a chance to redesign the playground? What needs does the playground have? Does it need a drinking fountain or more shade? What would make it more fun?

Explain that today they will imagine and design a playground that would fit in the same space. The only design constraint is that it must stay within the confines of school property. It does not have to look like a typical playground and could even extend to places such as the roof!

Students may work on this project individually, in pairs, or in groups. Students can write, draw, or do a combination of both.

Extension

Have students build a model of their designs or have groups choose a single design to build a model of. Students can vote on the winning design. They can use blocks or recycled/found materials.

Physics on the playground

The playground is the perfect place to investigate the fundamental concepts of physics! Sliding down the slide, swinging on the swing, and playing on seesaws show how pendulums, simple machines, and the laws of physics relate to real life.

Materials

- Timers
- Pencil

- Paper
- Various materials depending on the activity

Activities

- **Forces:** Investigate forces by performing a forces scavenger hunt. Ask students to find examples of different forces on the playground. Forces to look for include push (pushing a friend on a swing, tetherball), pull (pull-up or monkey bars), gravity (slide, jumping from the structure), and friction (slide, kicking a ball on the ground).
- **Simple Machines:** Look for simple machines and demonstrate them on the playground. Simple machines such as the inclined plane (slide, ramp); lever (seesaw or similar apparatus); wheel and axle (steering wheels, log rolls, rotating tic-tac-toe boards); pulley (if your school has a flagpole); screw (spiral fire pole, twisty slide). Have students make an informational video, pamphlet, 3D model, or poster to showcase examples of simple machines or forces on the playground or in the schoolyard.
- **Friction:** Experiment with friction using slides. Try sliding down the slides on different materials to see if it changes the speed as you travel down the slide. Students can record their observations and discuss the results.
- **Pendulums:** Explore pendulums using swings! Pendulums are simply weights suspended by a string that moves back and forth with help from gravity. Try these experiments:
  - **Pendulum basics:** Have children start swinging and then stop pumping their legs. What happens? Is the maximum height that they go changing? Are they slowing down?
  - **Starting point experiment:** Have one student sit in the swing with their legs out (don't bend them). Have another student stand straight behind them and hold the swing. The person standing behind the swing lets go of the swing without pushing! The person standing should not move! Will the swing hit the person standing? If they did not push, the swing should not hit them because a pendulum will not swing past its starting point unless you add energy with a push or by pumping their legs.
  - **Experiment with different loads:** Have a child and an adult swing side by side at the same rate. Once you are swinging simultaneously, stop pumping your legs and let the swing go back and forth naturally. What happens? Do they stay together?

- **Investigate rate:** Will a swing make the same number of oscillations no matter who is on it? Use a one-minute timer and have groups of students swing for one minute, counting how many times they return to the end. Have a partner pull them back and let them go. Record the number and switch. Partners or groups can try swinging "fast" with a big push or slower with a slight push. Does it make a difference? The number will be the same if the length of the swings is the same. The height that the swing starts at (amplitude) does not affect the rate.

Investigating snowflakes

While most students are familiar with snowflakes, few think about their unique geometry! This activity is best done when it is actively snowing. Dryer, fine snow works best to see the geometric crystals. But all snow reveals intricate crystal patterns and geometric shapes when examined closely!

Materials

- *Snowflake Bentley* by Jacqueline Briggs Martin and/or other books about snowflakes
- Magnifying glasses for each student or pair of students
- Dark pieces of cloth stretched and taped onto firm pieces of cardboard to "catch" snowflakes on
- Laminated paper
- Dry-erase writing utensils

NOTE For best results, it must be snowing to do this activity. Dry, small, flaked snow is best for observing crystal shapes. Freshly fallen, undisturbed snow can also work, but the crystals may be broken or combined with others.

Activity

Introduce the activity by reading the book *Snowflake Bentley* aloud to the class. Then explain that they will catch and observe snowflakes with a magnifying glass. Model making a tally chart to record the number of snowflakes for each number of points. Students can also try drawing snowflakes. Compare and discuss their observations as a whole class. What number of points had the most snowflakes? The least? What was the most unique snowflake they saw?

Outdoor Learning Tip: Winter in the Schoolyard

Outdoor instruction does not need to stop in the winter! While winter can provide some challenges to getting outside, it is also the time of year that fresh air, exercise, and daylight can be extremely beneficial to students and teachers! Winter also provides ice, snow, and cold that provide different learning opportunities and sensory experiences.

Variations

- Have students describe a selected snowflake with words. Students can list attributes and write 1–2 sentences or an entire paragraph.
- Consider having students write haikus or another form of poetry featuring the fascinating world of snowflakes!

Additional books about snowflakes:

- *Snowflakes in Photographs* by W. A. Bentley (These are the actual photographs that Bentley took and on which the picture book *Snowflake Bentley* by Jacqueline Briggs Martin is based. While not a children's book, the photos are fascinating and beautiful.)
- *The Story of Snow: The Science of Winter's Wonder* by Jon Nelson
- *The Secret Life of a Snowflake: An Up-Close Look at the Art and Science of Snowflakes* by Kenneth Libbrecht
- *Curious About Snow* by Gina Shaw (best for younger students)

How much water is in the snow?

Volume, density, and ratios come alive with this simple experiment comparing how much water you get from a set unit of snow. Students are always surprised about how little water you get from such a large quantity of snow! The general estimate is that one inch of rain equals approximately 12 inches of snow.

Materials

- A container that is the same size on top as on the bottom and will hold water for each pair of students in your class
- Ruler
- Notebook
- Pencil

- Paper towels or cloth to put under the container to absorb any condensation
- Enough snow to collect and fill containers
- Plastic wrap to prevent evaporation if extra time is needed for melting

NOTE This is a two-part activity. It takes time for the snow in the containers to melt. Start the experiment and collect the snow in the morning so that you can finish the experiment in the afternoon. If the snow has not melted in time, cover the tops of the containers with plastic wrap to minimize evaporation overnight.

Activity

Tell students you heard a weather forecaster say that an inch of rain equals approximately 12 inches of snow! Today, they are going to help you figure out if that estimate is accurate or not! Hand out a container for each pair of students and have students measure and record the height of the container. They should also guess how much (measurement in inches or centimeters) water will be at the bottom of their container after it melts and record it in their notebook.

Next, have students put on their winter gear and head outside to fill their containers. They should fill the containers to the very top, packing them in a bit. Have students observe the snow. Is it light and fluffy? Wet and heavy? Are the crystals small and dry or big and icy? They can add these observations to their notebook when they return inside.

Bring the containers indoors and place them in a flat, out-of-the-way area to melt. Make sure students record their observations about the snow in their notebooks before moving on to the next activity.

Periodically check on the snow and see how it is progressing. When the snow has melted, have students measure the height of the water and record this number and the ratio of snow to water that they found. For example, if the container held 5 inches of snow and they had ½ or .5 inches of snow, the ratio is 5 inches of snow to .5 inches of water/rain. Then they can compare the ratio they found to the weather forecasters' estimate using division.

Weather forecaster's ratio

1 divided by 12 = .084

.5 divided by 5 = .1

Notice these ratios are fairly close. Have your students calculate the ratio, record their answers, and compare their results. Were they greater than, less than, or about the same as the weather forecaster's estimated ratio? Have them discuss with their partner their results and make some conclusions about the results. If your results were different from the weather forecaster's, what do you think caused the difference?

Compare and share results as a class. Whose estimate do they think is more accurate? The weather forecaster's result or their result? Why?

Extension

Students may wish to repeat this activity using different types of snow and see how the ratio differs.

Writing

The writing activities in this section can be done in nearly any schoolyard. They are simple and do not require any special equipment.

Cloud Stories

When children observe the clouds and add in a little imagination, the most amazing stories emerge! All this activity requires is a day with clouds.

Materials

- Paper
- Pencil
- A day with interesting clouds

Activity

Ask students to observe the clouds for at least five minutes. What shapes do they see? Are there animals, castles, boats, or monsters? They can take notes or make quick sketches of their observations if they like. Sketches can be useful when writing their stories because cloud shapes can change rapidly, and they may want to look at their notes or drawings for further inspiration for their stories.

Next, explain that they will be using these observations as the starting point for a story. They can use some or all of their observations to develop a story. For example, if they saw clouds shaped like a dragon and a piece of popcorn, they may imagine a story about a dragon that loves popcorn and travels from village to village in search of every last morsel he can find. This activity can be done alone or in pairs.

Adjusting the activity

Beginning writers can write observations or a sentence or two describing what they saw.

Variations

Students can observe clouds and the shapes they see for a longer period, drawing and chronicling the changes. Then based on the observations, they can write a story that connects all the different objects they saw in the story!

Pair this activity with a book appropriate for your students, such as *Cloud Boy* by Rhode Montijo; *It Looked Like Spilt Milk* by Charles G. Shaw; *The Cloud Book* by Tomie dePaola; *Little Cloud* by Eric Carle; and *The Cloud Spinner* by Michael Catchpool.

Procedural writing on the playground

The playground is perfect for students to practice procedural writing. Students enjoy being the expert and instructing others on how to do something! If you do not have a playground, have children focus on writing about what they do in the schoolyard (games, jump rope, etc.).

Materials

- Pencil
- Paper
- How-to books to use as mentor texts
- Access to the playground or other activities that children can write a how-to about

Activity

Procedural writing, often called a "how-to," is a form of expository writing. In this form of writing, students must teach the reader how to do something through their writing. For this activity, students will select something that can be done on the playground and write a how-to. These examples can be typical playground activities such as going down the slide or more advanced playground "tricks" such as doing a flip on a bar or climbing up to a special spot.

Before your writers start writing, model what this type of writing can look like by reading aloud a mentor text.

Some favorites are:

- *How to Wash a Woolly Mammoth* by Michelle Robinson
- *How to Read a Story* by Kate Messner
- *How to Make Friends with a Ghost* by Rebecca Green
- *How to Catch a Unicorn* by Adam Wallace (series)
- *How to Feed Your Parents* by Ryan Miller

After reading a mentor text or two and discussing common features of how-to books, children may head to the playground to decide on their topics. Have them get to work immediately on their writing after choosing. It may take more than one visit to the playground to finish their rough drafts. Consider having children take or draw pictures to add to their writing. You can have children revise and complete the other stages of the writing process in the classroom or outdoors.

Final Thoughts

The schoolyard is an easy-to-access resource that offers an array of learning opportunities. After practicing math, playing word games, and writing how-to books on the school grounds, it is time to take your class on a learning adventure outside the schoolyard. In the next chapter, you will learn how to use the neighborhood near your school in your outdoor lessons.

03 Visiting the Neighborhood

After the schoolyard, the neighborhood is the second most accessible outdoor space available to most teachers. In this book, the neighborhood refers to the area within walking distance of your school. While often overlooked as an instructional resource, the neighborhood can offer your students a rich array of outdoor learning experiences.

The resources available in the neighborhood for any particular school are highly context-sensitive. The key is to inventory what resources you have in your school's neighborhood or area near your school and select the activities that work best for your setting. For example, urban schools are able to use houses, buildings, streets, and stores surrounding their school as opportunities to utilize environmental print such as street and business signs. Urban environments are also great for studying how numbers and shapes are used in context, and for studying urban trees.

While there are activities in this chapter that can be done at a school in a rural setting, if your school is located far outside of town, some of the activities assuming an urban setting will require more planning and a field trip. However, your school likely has different opportunities based on your location and may be able to implement activities that normally would require travel to a park directly on the school grounds! Check out chapter 5, Farther Afield, for activities you may be able to do nearby your school and plan some of the activities in this chapter as your "farther afield" activities.

In this chapter, you will find sections focusing on walking adventures, utilizing urban trees, and how to use the neighborhood to inspire writing. Walking adventures are a great way to begin exploring and learning in the neighborhood near your school. These activities help children use the neighborhood to practice and apply skills learned in the classroom, such as geometric shapes, measurement, and phonics.

Street trees are an often overlooked learning resource and are usually available even in highly urbanized areas (although the density and distribution of street trees in our cities are unfortunately not equitable). Investigating the number and types of trees they find that grow in the neighborhood can be fascinating. Students are often surprised by the diversity!

The neighborhood also serves as a source of inspiration for writers, for example, when imagining what exists beyond a door or creating pamphlets or advertisements to encourage people to visit their neighborhood. These projects can also help your students build connections and a sense of pride in their community.

Walking Adventures

A walking adventure gives your students tasks such as searching for arrays or words with vowel teams to complete while walking around the neighborhood. These walks are a simple way to get your class outside and help them see how math and written language are everywhere! Walking adventures also provide children with new experiences that build background knowledge, which is key for reading comprehension and helps develop oral language and observation skills (see Figure 3.1). Most walks require few materials beyond a pencil and a notebook! These activities can be done in any season.

Math walks

This section will help your students notice how math is all around us, particularly in their school neighborhood. They get students moving and actively looking for math in the real world! Math walks are a simple way to take your class outdoors in any season while reinforcing target math skills.

Geometry walks

Shapes are all around us! Often, we do not notice how important shapes and geometry are until we start looking closer. More developed environments offer many examples of shapes in architecture and other structures. Your students will likely be surprised just how important geometry is in the design of buildings and structures when they start looking closely. Shapes can also be found in the natural world. Your students may be surprised to find these math concepts in nature and delight in finding examples!

Materials

- Pencil
- Small ruler (to assist in drawing shapes)

Outdoor Learning Tip: Portable Writing Surfaces

Clipboards make great portable writing surfaces for learning outside. If you do not have a class set of clipboards, you can easily make your own clipboards using stiff cardboard cut to size and attaching a binder clip to the top. The binder clip acts as the "clip" to hold papers in place. You can also place binder clips on a student whiteboard or chalkboard, allowing them to serve as a clipboard.

Figure 3.1 Bridge walk: Students exploring their neighborhood in Brooklyn, New York
Source: Andrew Chiappetta

- Notebook or paper
- Clipboard
- Optional: *City Shapes* by Diana Murray
- For advanced variations: protractor, compass, measuring tape

Activity

The picture book *City Shapes* by Diana Murray is the perfect introduction to this activity, particularly for younger students. Before heading out, read the suggested picture book aloud and/or explain to your class that today they will be walking around the neighborhood looking for shapes. Lead a quick discussion with your students. **Questions you may want to pose:** What shapes do you think you will find the most of as you walk around the neighborhood today? Record some of their answers on chart paper to compare their findings afterward.

Lead your class on a walk through the neighborhood looking for geometric shapes. Have your class walk in a single line if students are working individually, or a double line if they are working in pairs. Make stops to observe and look for shapes along the route (see Figures 3.2 and 3.3). Ask your students to keep track of the number and type of shapes they find in a notebook. Encourage them to look for shapes that are part of a larger shape, such as windows in a large rectangular building, or the triangle portion of the roof of a house. Once they start looking, they will be amazed at all the shapes they find!

Figure 3.2 Look at all the rectangles and squares on buildings and the triangles on the crane
Source: Rachel Tidd

Outdoor Learning Tips: Math Walks in Natural Environments

While the math walks in this chapter focus on more developed areas, many of these walks can also be done in natural areas. If you have access to or plan to visit more natural areas, have your students do the same walk looking for examples of math concepts in nature. Angles, shapes, examples of numbers (three petals on a flower), and spirals are all ways math can be seen in nature.

Figure 3.3 This utility hole is a great example of a circle. It is also surrounded by square tiles.
Source: Rachel Tidd

You may wish for them to make a tally chart or graph of the shapes. They can also choose one or two shapes to investigate further by recording the number of sides, measuring the sides (or diameter), and sketching the shape. Each student can record the shapes they find, or they can work in pairs.

After the walk, ask the students in your class to share what shape they saw the most. Make a quick tally chart compiling their class data. You may wish to discuss questions such as, How does the data compare to your predictions? Did anything surprise you during the walk? Did you see more of certain shapes than you expected?

Variations

- **Angle hunt:** For an angle walk have your students bring protractors and measure angles they find in the neighborhood. Sidewalk cracks, bricks, gates, playground structures, and more are all interesting places to discover angles (see Figure 3.4). See if they can find at least four different angle measurements. Have them record the measurement of the angle, where it was located (e.g. the metal railing), and geographic location (e.g. 254 State Street). Have them compare and discuss results in groups or a whole group.
- **Symmetry search:** Have students look for shapes containing at least one line of symmetry. Can they find shapes with two, three, or more

Figure 3.4 Measuring the angles between rocks on a retaining wall
Source: Rachel Tidd

lines of symmetry? They should record an example of each shape and its lines of symmetry in their notebooks. Have students work in pairs and spread out along the street, allowing each group enough space to look for shapes for a few minutes. Then move to a different street to look for more symmetrical shapes. Have them share some examples!

- **Circumference hunt:** Ask students to search for two or three examples of circles. They should measure and record the diameter of the circle, the general location (e.g. on a sign), and the geographic location/ address. Then have them calculate the circumference.

Number walks

Number-themed walks ask your students to search for specific categories of numbers, such as decimals, even and odd numbers, or to round all the numbers found. This is a great activity that you can adapt and use to reinforce many different math skills and grade levels. If your school is in a more rural area or on a campus, there are still numbers to be found if you look closely! One of the best places is the license plates in the school parking lot.

Materials

- Pencil
- Notebook or paper
- Clipboard

Activity

Here is a description of a number walk for your youngest students. For advanced students, see the following variations listed. You can adjust number walks for varying grade levels by changing what kind of numbers students look for.

Lead your class on a walk looking for numbers (see Figure 3.5). Ask students to record all the numbers they see in their notebooks. This activity is best done individually with each student recording their own numbers. Lead a class discussion about what students found and noticed and how numbers are used in the neighborhood to wrap up the activity.

Other numbers you may ask them to look for

- What is the largest and smallest number they can find?
- Can they find a number in the ones, tens, hundreds, or thousands? Larger?
- Can they find a number with an 8 in the tens place?

Figure 3.5 These parking signs have numbers written in words and numerals

Source: Rachel Tidd

Variations

- **Even and odd numbers:** Ask students to make two columns on their paper and label one column *even* and one *odd*. As they spot numbers, have them record and identify if the number is even or odd, and record it in the correct column. After the walk, lead a discussion about what students noticed about even and odd numbers and how they are used. Are even or odd numbers more common? Did they notice how even and odd numbers are used on the street (usually odd numbers are on the left, even on the right)?
- **Rounding:** Ask students to round numbers to a specified place value. For example, for the first five minutes of a walk have children round the numbers they see to the nearest ten. Then for the next five minutes, have children round the numbers they see to the nearest

hundred. Have them record both the original number and the rounded number in their notebook. Lead a discussion about their findings.

- **Comparing numbers:** Designate a number and have students compare all the numbers they see in the neighborhood to the designated number. They should write both numbers and use a greater than, less than, or equal sign symbol to compare the designated number to the found number.
- **Running total:** Have students calculate a running total of ten numbers that they see in the neighborhood. They should record each step in their notebooks.
- **Decimals:** How are decimals used in the neighborhood? This is often easier in a location with stores and businesses in the area. Common places that decimals are used are gas stations, signs, prices, distances, etc. Lead a discussion about when and where decimals are used. Why or when are they useful?
- **Time:** While walking around the neighborhood, children can practice telling time by carrying small clocks (the kind used in the classroom to learn how to tell time). Every so often stop and either have them show the current time or give them a time to show on the clock. You can also have students calculate elapsed time. This can be a great add-on activity or when walking to another destination!

Finding arrays and groups

Real-life arrays (objects, numbers, shapes, or pictures arranged in rows and columns) or examples of things that come in groups are everywhere! This activity will open your students' eyes to how this multiplication concept can be found in a surprising number of places around the neighborhood!

Materials

- Pencil
- Notebook or paper
- Clipboard

Activity

If needed, introduce the idea of an array and how it relates to multiplication to your students and discuss or model a few examples. Then lead your class on a walk through the neighborhood. Explain that they will be looking for examples of arrays. Some examples of arrays they may see in the neighborhood are windows on the side of a building, panes of glass in a window, cars parked along the road, paving stones on a walkway, tile patterns, or flowers planted in rows (see Figures 3.6, 3.7, and 3.8).

After pointing out a few examples as you walk, ask your students to record each example. They can draw or write a description and the multiplication fact that each array represents.

Variations

- Repeat the activity looking for things that occur in groups. For example, five daisies growing in each bunch, three benches, four swings on each swing set, six windows on each car, or five petals on each flower. They should draw each example and calculate the total.
- Students in the lower grades can draw and discuss the arrays that they find.

Skip counting walk

Skip counting is an important and useful skill for students to learn. Learning and practicing more advanced skip counting patterns, such as 4s, 6s, and 9s,

Figure 3.6 This grate is an excellent example of an array
Source: Rachel Tidd

Figure 3.7 This building has a giant array of circles on the front
Source: Rachel Tidd

Figure 3.8 Students looking at the many examples of arrays on
the structure of the Brooklyn Bridge
Source: Andrew Chiappetta

will also help your students become more fluent with multiplication facts. A skip counting walk is a great way to incorporate movement and outdoor time into the school day and practice skip counting.

Materials

- Chalk

Activity

Take your class for a walk through the neighborhood (or even around school property). While walking, lead the class through a skip counting sequence and pair it with a movement. For example, count by fives and hop for each number, or count by twos and punch twice toward the sky. After a few rounds, choose a student to lead the group.

Variation

Locate stairs that your students are allowed to write on with chalk. There should be enough room for each group of students to do this activity simultaneously. Have each group write a different skip counting sequence going up the stairs using chalk. Then have the students in each group line up in front of their number sequence. Students take turns hopping up each stair while chanting the number sequence. When they reach the top, have them turn around and hop back down while counting backward! When they have finished, they move to the back of the line of the adjacent group (and a different number sequence). If your class has difficulty with or has just learned a new number sequence, have all the groups work on the same number sequence.

Measuring distances

Estimating distance can be difficult for students because they often lack experience using distances in real life. This activity will help your students gain hands-on experience with various distances by personally measuring them. This will give them a personal reference they can draw upon when estimating distances in the future.

Materials

- Pencil
- Notebook or paper
- Clipboard
- Measuring tape or yard/meter stick
- Optional for variation: measuring/trundle wheel

Activity

Divide your students into pairs or groups. Each group should have a measuring tape or yard/meter stick. Before your students begin measuring, have them choose three locations and estimate how far they think each destination is from the starting point. They will work together using the measuring stick or tape end over end to measure the distance. Have students measure each distance and record them in their notebooks. Afterward, have students share their results and reflections.

Possible topics to bring up during the reflection discussion

- Were their estimates close to the actual distance or were they way off?
- Did they over- or underestimate?
- What surprised them?
- Did the groups have different results? Why might that have happened?

Variations

- **Steps:** Try the same activity but have students count steps. Have students measure the number of steps to the same locations. Afterward, have students share their results and compare them to other groups. Record each group's step number on chart paper so the whole group can see the data. What do they notice? Why do the numbers vary? Are steps a good way to measure distance?
- **Measuring wheel or trundle:** If you have access to measuring or trundle wheels, it can be fun for children to repeat these activities using this tool and compare the results (see Figure 3.9). Which method do they think is more accurate? Which is easier to use?
- **Converting units:** Have more advanced students convert the distances to different units. Convert measurements to kilometers, meters, centimeters, inches, and feet.

Reading and writing walks

Noticing words and recognizing print patterns such as common letter combinations, syllables, and morphemes is foundational for learning to read. Environmental print found in the neighborhood is a useful resource to apply these skills by looking for phonics patterns, practicing writing words, and creating maps in a real-world context. This section shows you how to use words in your neighborhood to reinforce phonics, spelling, and writing skills.

Figure 3.9 Using a trundle wheel to measure distances
Source: Rachel Tidd

Words in our neighborhood

Words are everywhere on town, city, and neighborhood streets! This activity is similar to "write the room" activities usually completed inside the classroom. Looking for letters, phonemes, words, or phonics patterns in the neighborhood helps your students increase their awareness of the words around them. You may focus on different phonics patterns, spelling rules, or categories that are relevant for your students, for variety, or to differentiate the activity.

Materials

- Pencil
- Notebook or paper
- Clipboard
- Chart paper or something to record student findings for display and discussion

Activity

Lead your students on a walk to look for and record words they see in the neighborhood! Have them record each word found in their notebooks. You can discover words together or as a whole group. You can also have your students find and record words on their own (or in pairs) in a specified area.

After the walk, discuss the words they found. If desired, you can make a huge list of all the words that your students found. Some questions you may wish to ask them might be, What kinds of words were the most common? Labels? Signs? Other? Why are words helpful in the neighborhood? What would happen if there were no words? No street signs?

Variations

- **Word sort:** Sort the found words into categories. Have students look at their words and decide on ways they could organize or sort them. Do words have similar letter patterns, beginning sounds, or ending sounds? What about different categories of words, such as words used on road signs, in advertising, warnings, street signs, etc.?
- **Street names:** Lead a walk having students focus on recording street signs. This can be a great way to focus on one category of environmental print without overwhelming beginning writers. Additional categories to consider are signs, business names, or building names.
- **Phonics pattern:** Go on a scavenger hunt to find examples of particular phonics skills your students are learning. Look at signs, ads, car brands, and other environmental print for examples of silent E words (fire, drive, ahead), vowel teams (street, road, speed, school), R-controlled vowels (park, meter), multisyllable words (hydrant, ticket, limit), suffixes (parking, closed), and more!
- **Block play:** Consider taking pictures or adding laminated labels with business, building, and street signs from the school neighborhood and adding them to the block area. This can inspire some amazing block play based on your neighborhood walks!
- **Letters or sounds:** Students can look for letters or sounds and then copy the letter or draw a picture of where they saw it.

Finding small bits of nature in unexpected places

Small bits of wild can be found anywhere, even in urban locations. In this activity, students will learn to look closely for small or unexpected examples of nature in the school's neighborhood.

Materials

- A book about nature in urban areas or unexpected places (see box)
- Pencil

Suggested Read-alouds Featuring Nature in Unexpected Places

- *Weeds Find a Way* by Cindy Jenson-Elliott
- *Finding Wild* by Megan Wagner Lloyd
- *Outside In* by Deborah Underwood
- *Jayden's Impossible Garden* by Mélina Mangal
- *Wild City: Meet the Animals Who Share Our City Spaces* by Ben Hoare
- *Falcons in the City: The Story of a Peregrine Family* by Chris Earley
- *City Hawk: The Story of Pale Male* by Meghan McCarthy
- *A Green Place to Be: The Creation of Central Park* by Ashley Benham Yazdani
- *Nature in the Neighborhood* by Gordon Morrison

- Notebook or paper
- Clipboard

Activity

To introduce the idea of small bits of nature, begin with a read-aloud featuring nature in unexpected places.

After reading the book take your class on a walk to look for bits of nature in surprising or unexpected places. What new bits of nature are revealed when looking at the neighborhood through this new lens?

Depending on the age and abilities of your students, you may ask students to

- Draw and write a sentence or a few sentences describing what they found.
- Write a paragraph describing the bit of nature in detail, the location, and why they think it is important.

Wrap up the lesson by having students share their work and discuss why these small bits of nature might be important.

Extension

Have students look for bits of nature at different times of the year and/ or in different locations. Have them write a new paragraph describing what they found for each trip. After several walks, they can compile their writing into a book showcasing nature in the neighborhood. A great mentor text for this activity is *Nature in the Neighborhood* by Gordon Morrison. This story highlights examples of nature in a neighborhood through the seasons. It also integrates scientific facts about plants and animals, which could be an excellent way to incorporate science standards.

Mapping the neighborhood

Mapmaking helps children build spatial reasoning skills and make sense of the world around them. Learning to read a map is an important skill even in the digital age! Plan several walks focusing on different aspects of the neighborhood and have students add more details to their maps during each session. Locations such as a street or several streets, school grounds, the whole neighborhood, a main street, or a nearby park all work well for this project.

Materials

- Large pieces of paper for the map
- Paper or notebook for sketches and notes
- Pencils
- Colored pencils
- Clipboards
- Rulers
- Examples of maps
- Compass for labeling directions
- Optional: use digital cameras or tablets with cameras to take pictures to use as a reference if you plan on working on maps in the classroom

Activity

Depending on your students' familiarity with maps, you may wish to begin this activity by examining and comparing different kinds of maps. What do they have in common? What information do they show?

Explain to your class that they will make a map of the neighborhood, street, park, or school grounds. Walk through the area together to get a feel for it. Then walk through the area again, but this time have students look for specific features or landmarks in the area. As students walk around the area a second time, they should make quick sketches and notes on paper or in a notebook about the important features and landmarks they see. If you have access to digital cameras, have your students take pictures of the area to refer to later if working on their map back in the classroom.

Children can then begin working on a rough outline of their maps while still at the location. This rough draft will be used to make a larger map in the classroom (or outside, if you prefer). Make sure they add important labels such as street names, buildings, and directions (use a compass).

Once your students have drawn their maps, have them begin working on a larger map. Make sure they do this work in pencil to allow for modifications. You may have your students work individually or in small groups. Because of the larger paper size, you may find that this part of the project works best when done on tables or even indoors on the floor. Your students will use their rough draft outlines and memory to sketch the basic features of the map on large paper.

Depending on how detailed you would like the final maps to be and how much class time you devote to the project, schedule several additional walks focusing on a specific element each time. For example, for the first walk, you may have students focus on drawing the outline of all the streets and labeling them with their names. On subsequent walks, you can have your students focus on locating major landmarks such as parks, landmarks, and important buildings and labeling them in the correct location on their maps. You may wish to plan additional walks focusing on specific elements such as trees, parking, stores, and signs.

When your students have finished adding details to their maps, have them outline the pencil in black marker or a black colored pencil, add color, a compass rose, and a legend. If these map features are new to your students, introduce them one at a time and have everyone add them to their map.

Adjusting the Activity

- **To scale:** Students in the upper grades can make their map using a scale. This will require measuring distance physically or using a map or resource such as Google Maps. Constructing and using a scale is an excellent way for students to practice and use ratios in real life!

Variation

- **3D model:** If you are lucky enough to have wooden unit blocks in your classroom, have students construct a model of the neighborhood.

They can add to the model as they learn and notice new details. Older students often enjoy using smaller blocks such as Lego or Keva planks. If you don't have unit blocks, you can also have students build a model using recycled materials, paper, and other materials. Building models is a great way for students to visualize and synthesize information they have learned through different activities in the neighborhood.

Our friends the trees

Trees are an often overlooked natural resource, which makes them a perfect subject for students to study. While teaching in New York City, my students and I discovered the vast array of city tree species planted there! Most people do not realize that a forester or arborist manages the tree species in many towns and cities. The activities in this section can be combined to create a long-term unit study on trees.

Leaf guide

Children find leaves fascinating. Learning to identify common tree species by their shape and physical features helps children build their knowledge of the natural world while developing research and writing skills, learning scientific classification, and practicing observation skills. This leaf guide project can be a stand-alone activity or can be combined with the tree inventory or tree tour guide.

Materials

- Tree field guides for the local geographical area (at least one guide for each group)
- Leaf samples collected by students
- Glue
- Materials for preferred preservation method
- Colored pencils

Activity

Take your class on a walk and have them collect 5–10 different tree leaves. Explain that they will identify each tree's species and use them to create a leaf guidebook (see Figure 3.10). Remind children to collect leaves that have already fallen from the tree when possible.

The leaf book will feature one page for each leaf, the tree's species, the leaf's critical features (lobes, points, vein patterns, edge patterns), and any other information they would like to include.

Figure 3.10 A student working on a leaf book
Source: Rachel Tidd

If you would like children to use the actual leaves in their book (versus just a drawing of the leaf), you can place leaves between the pages of a heavy book, so they remain flat. Fresh leaves become brittle and curl when they dry out, so pressing them will make it easier to glue or tape into a book. You can also have children preserve the leaves by pressing them between wax paper. Place a towel on top of the wax paper and use a warm iron on top of the towel. This will coat the leaves in a thin coating of wax and help preserve them. Leaves can also be laminated or pressed between contact paper (see Figure 3.11).

Adjusting the activity

- Create a template of a leaf guide page to scaffold this activity for students who require more in writing support.
- You may wish students to include important nonfiction features such as a table of contents, diagrams with labels, and a glossary in their books.
- Have older students include the scientific names and add more details about the trees that each leaf comes from to their books.

Figure 3.11 Examples of student leaf books
Source: Rachel Tidd

Leaf shape resources

Leaf shapes and characteristics are often found at the beginning of field guides.

Upper grade students may like this detailed chart by the *Central Yukon Species Inventory Project* found at https://www.flora.dempstercountry.org/Leaf.Glossary.html

Britannica Kids has a simple diagram of a leaf. You can find it at https://kids.britannica.com/kids/article/leaf/433080

My tree through the year

Choosing a tree, learning more about it, and watching it change over time can be a special experience for a child. By the end of this project, students will be an expert on their tree and showcase their newfound knowledge with an accordion-style book.

Materials

- Tree guides and other books about trees for research
- Paper/clipboard or notebook
- Pencil
- Colored pencils

- Tape
- Paper for making the accordion book
- Measuring tape

Activity

For this activity, students will choose a street tree and visit the tree several times over the school year, observing how it changes. Students will create an accordion that features drawings and observations of the tree. After each observation students will add another page to the accordion. Each page will feature a drawing of the tree and a paragraph (or sentence) describing their observations. You may also wish students to add a page featuring any information learned about the tree through research. Since this is an ongoing project, you will need to collect and store the pages until the final observation page is added.

First visit: selecting a tree

Take the class to an area where there are many street trees. Ask each student to select a tree. Explain that they will learn about this tree and visit it throughout the year.

Students should make careful observations about the tree and record them (see Figure 3.12). They should record leaf shape and bark texture. They can measure the circumference of the trunk and record it. They should also include sketches of the whole tree, leaves, and bark, making their drawings and notes as detailed as possible. This will help them identify the tree or confirm their identification using a field guide.

After making their initial observations, have children use field guides to identify the tree species and learn more about them. Have them create a page for their accordion that includes a detailed picture of their tree and a paragraph describing their observations below it (see Figure 3.13). You may wish to have students work on their book pages on-site or back in the classroom. This project's level of detail and complexity can be adjusted to fit your students' needs.

Follow-up visits later in the year

Visit their trees at least once each season. Have students write observations and draw a detailed picture of the tree for each visit. They should note any changes since their last visit and have the children create another page for their accordion book. It should include a drawing of the tree's appearance and a sentence or paragraph describing what they saw and any changes they noticed.

Figure 3.12 Students from The Brooklyn New School observing
and drawing trees
Source: Andrew Chiappetta

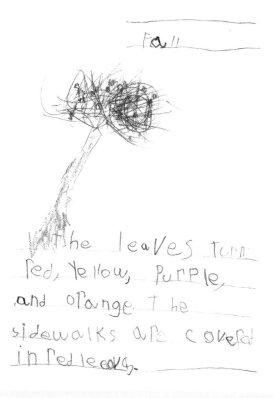

Fall

The leaves turn
red, yellow, purple,
and orange. The
sidewalks are covered
in red leaves.

Figure 3.13 Example of a drawing for the tree accordion book
Source: Rachel Tidd

Assembling the book

You can have students add additional pages to the accordions as you go or assemble the entire accordion book after the final visit. To attach pages with a bendable seam, lay pages next to each other. Make sure the edges are touching but not overlapping. Place a long strip of tape over the area where the pages meet.

They will also need to make the starting page or cover for the accordion book (see Figure 3.14). It should include the title and the author of the project, as well as an illustration of the tree.

Figure 3.14 Example cover of an accordion book featuring a Sugar Maple tree
Source: Rachel Tidd

Books About Trees

Here are some favorite books about trees for the classroom. Adding books about trees to the classroom library will create excitement for their tree projects and encourage them to learn more about trees. Getting a few kids interested can often inspire others to look at and read about trees. The enthusiasm becomes contagious!

- *The Sibley Guide to Trees* by David Allen Sibley
- *Peterson First Guide to Trees* by George A. Petrides
- *Can You Hear the Trees Talking? Discovering the Hidden Life of the Forest* by Peter Wohlleben
- *The Tree Book for Kids and Their Grown-Ups* by Gina Ingoglia
- *The Magic and Mystery of Trees* by Jen Green
- *A Tree Is a Home* by Pamela Hickman
- *DK Eyewitness Books: Tree: Discover the Fascinating World of Trees from Tiny Seeds to Mighty Forest Giants* by David Burnie
- *Trees, Leaves, Flowers, and Seeds: A Visual Encyclopedia of the Plant Kingdom* by DK & Smithsonian Institution
- *Trees, Leaves and Bark* by Diane L. Burns
- *Dear Baobab* by Cheryl Foggo
- *The Tree Lady: The True Story of How One Tree Loving Lady Changed a City Forever* by H. Joseph Hopkins
- *Wangari's Trees of Peace: A True Story from Africa* by Jeanette Winter
- *Because of an Acorn* by Lola M. Schaefer
- *The Magic and Mystery of Trees* by Jen Green
- *Be a Tree!* by Maria Gianferrari

Variations

- **A tree is a home:** Look for signs of animals, insects, lichen, and other living things that make their home in their tree. Students may wish to learn more about them and add this information to their books.
- **Further research:** Research optimal growing conditions for their tree. Do they think the tree will do well in its current location? Why or why not?
- **Meditation:** Have them sit by their tree and meditate or tune into how the tree makes them feel. Have them touch the trunk and take a few minutes to reflect. Does the tree make them feel calmer? Peaceful? Do they feel they are friends with their tree? Ask them to journal their thoughts, feelings, and reflections on their tree.

Tree arborist or expert

Having an expert visit your classroom can be an amazing experience for your students. Many cities have a city forester or arborist. If you live in a small town, consider asking a local tree arborist, tree surgeon, forester, landscape architect, or another person who works with, maintains, or studies trees in your community to speak to your class about trees and what role trees play in their job. Often city arborists or other tree experts are also willing to give your class a tour of trees! It never hurts to inquire.

Materials

- Chart paper or another way to record student questions
- Marker
- Community expert relating to trees to visit the class

Activity

Brainstorm together and, if needed, have students research the benefits of trees before the visit.

- Why are trees important?
- Why do we want trees in towns and cities?

To prepare for the expert's visit, lead a class brainstorming session, making a list of questions they would like to ask the expert when they visit. You may need to give them a little information on the person and their job to help guide their questions. Record these questions and review them before the visitor arrives. Display the questions for children to see during the visit to help them remember their questions.

Adjusting the activity

Have older students research different jobs relating to trees, such as an arborist, forester, landscaper, landscape architect, horticulturist, dendrologist, orchard manager, ecologist, environmental or forest engineer, paper scientist, and more. Have students research what the job responsibilities are, the education needed, and other details. Students or pairs of students can then give an informal presentation sharing their findings with the class.

Tree inventory

In this activity, students will learn to identify trees and become experts on the trees around their neighborhoods. Your students may be surprised at the variety of tree species they find!

Outdoor Learning Tip: Utilizing Community Voices and Resources

Inviting community members and experts into the classroom is not just for the youngest grades. If you and your class discover interesting places, shops, historical landmarks, and parks, consider asking community members or experts associated with them to speak to your class about the topic. Learning from local experts expands children's knowledge and experience as well as deepens their connection to the community and strengthens their sense of place.

Most students are unfamiliar with occupations outside basic categories (doctor, teacher, lawyer, shop clerk). By bringing community members into the classroom, you are showing them the variety of career opportunities that exist. Often these connections can lead to unique field trip opportunities for your class. They can also have cross-curricular connections; for example, visiting the town or city court and talking to a judge can connect to a unit on government.

Local people to consider inviting might be a local historian, owner of a local historic house; local gardening expert to talk about local plants or gardens; community garden director; local store owner; a reporter from a newspaper, radio, or other media outlet; city or park forester; government officials such as judges, mayors, council members; and more.

Selecting a Location for Exploring Trees

While street trees are used as an example, any area with trees would work for this activity. Consider school grounds, nearby parks, edges of property, fields, or parks, or use multiple streets if there are only a few trees per street. You may want to scout out potential areas beforehand. Check to ensure the selected location has enough trees and several different species.

Materials

- Tree field guides based on your geographical area (at least one guide for each group)
- Notebook or paper/clipboard
- Pencil
- Colored pencils
- Simple map of the area selected either drawn or printed/copied where students can plot their trees
- One "class map" where each group's tree can be added
- Optional: cameras or tablets for taking pictures of trees

Activity

Explain that a tree inventory counts, identifies, and shows the location of each tree in a specified area. City foresters often create maps of all the trees in the whole city or town.

Explain to your class that they will take an inventory of street trees today. Each group will work together to identify one to two trees. Working in pairs, have students choose a street tree to identify using a tree guide. Ask them to record the common name, species, and important facts about the tree. They should also sketch a picture of the whole tree, the bark, and a leaf. Students should use the map provided to locate their tree and place a point on their map to show its location. Students can also describe the tree's features using words. They should also record the location of the tree using the nearest address. Have students select a second tree and repeat the process if there are enough trees in the area. If you have digital cameras or devices with a camera available, have students take pictures of the trees.

Afterward, have students come together and ask each group to share the species of tree(s) they found, mention a noteworthy fact, and add their tree to the class map. Make a class list of all the different types of trees the students identified and the total number of trees.

Adjusting the activity

Provide students with a packet of information limited to only the tree types that they are likely to encounter. Make your own or print/photocopy pages from a beginner's tree guide. This will make it easier for them to identify the tree species. A simple worksheet that lists each fact you would like them to find and provides boxes for sketches can also help scaffold the activity for different levels.

Variations

- **Class book:** Have each group create a page about their tree and create a class book.
- **Try another location:** Repeat the inventory activity in a different area and compare the results.
- **Wall display:** Place the class tree map on a bulletin board and have each student or pair write a paragraph about their tree. Hang the paragraphs around the map and use string to connect the paragraph to the tree's location on the map.

Tree tour

Having students create a tree tour is an excellent way to build on the tree inventory. This activity asks students to design a walking tour of different trees in the neighborhood, synthesize the information learned, and present it in a way that educates others. The information can be presented in a book, booklet, pamphlet, or audio tour format.

Materials

- Tree field guides based on your geographical area (at least one guide for each group)
- Notebook or paper/clipboard
- Pencil
- Colored pencils
- Simple map of the area selected, either made by the class during the tree inventory or a satellite image printed from an online website such as Google
- Materials for various project formats such as paper, booklets, stapler, or recording devices for audio tours

Optional materials

- Camera/s for taking images of specific trees
- Printer to print pictures to add to finished projects

Activity

Using the information from the tree inventory (or have students identify trees as part of this project), ask your students to select five neighborhood trees and then create an informational tour. They may choose to feature trees because of their size, species, location, or history. You will find that this activity is best done in small groups.

Ask students to write an introduction to the tour, describe the location, briefly describe each tree, and write a concluding paragraph. You may specify the number of trees and particular details to be included based on the grade level of your students and available class time to devote to the project.

Have your students select the format that they wish to present the tour in (or you can specify the method). Creating a booklet, pamphlet, or audio tour are excellent format options for this type of project. If students choose to create an audio tour, ensure they write the script first and that all members contribute to the recording.

Adjusting the activity

- Depending on the age and ability of your students, select an appropriate number of trees to profile for the tour to include. Adjust and define the information they should include.
- You can extend this activity by having students estimate the tree's age and size, and research when trees were planted or other historical facts about the trees (see Figure 3.15). For example, a huge oak tree may have existed when the town or city was founded or was planted in front of a building or house of significance.

Figure 3.15 Working together to measure a giant tree located in a neighborhood park
Source: Rachel Tidd

Writing and the neighborhood

The neighborhood around your school can be a fantastic way to inspire your writers! Taking writing out of the classroom provides your students with new experiences and environments to write about. It can be a springboard for new ideas and connections. Writing prompts using the neighborhood as the setting for a story, creating riddles, writing odes, practicing descriptive writing, and creating pamphlets and tour guides will encourage your students to view the area surrounding their school with a new perspective!

Outdoor Learning Tip: Nature Journaling

Nature journaling is diary-type entries made up of writing, drawing, and sometimes natural items taped to pages. Together with your students, you will chronicle observations of nature and combine science, writing, and art (see Figure 3.16). Nature journaling can be a great weekly or monthly writing routine for your class! It can be done anywhere there is a bit of nature. Nature journals also combine well with the sit spot activities in chapter 4. Journaling can be done directly in their notebook devoted to outdoor learning or in a separate notebook. For more information on creating one large classroom nature journal, see chapter 5. There are many resources and books about nature journaling including a free PDF download of the book *How to Teach Nature Journaling* by John Muir Laws and Emilie Lygren. You can find it at https://johnmuirlaws.com/journaling-curriculum/.

Figure 3.16 A student works on their nature journal
Source: Rachel Tidd

Descriptive writing

Capturing a person, place, emotion, or object through descriptive writing involves paying attention to detail and using as many of your senses as possible to describe the object. In this activity, students will choose a subject from the neighborhood environment to practice descriptive writing.

Materials

- Paper and clipboard or notebook
- Pencil

Activity

This activity assumes your students have already been introduced to descriptive writing. If this is a new style of writing for them, take time to introduce this type of writing and then move on to the lesson with the following exercise.

Allow students to choose an object, feature, person, or location in the neighborhood to be the focus of their descriptive writing. Remind them to use as many senses as possible when describing their chosen subject.

Example topics for descriptive writing in the neighborhood:

- A natural object such as a flower, tree, plant, rock, nut, animal, or bird
- Neighborhood objects such as a statue, mailbox, mural, sign, sidewalk, or bike rack
- A location such as a store, park, corner, bus stop, intersection, stoop, bus loop, bridge, empty lot, or playground
- Person in the neighborhood such as a crossing guard, street food seller, newsstand clerk, shopkeeper, park ranger, friendly neighbor, parking lot attendant, etc.

When your students have finished their writing, ask for a few volunteers to share their work with the class. They should not tell the class the subject that they were writing about. Instead, ask your class to listen and see if they can guess what the writer was describing. They can raise their hands if they would like to guess the subject of the writing.

Adjusting the activity

You can modify this assignment by changing the amount of writing required. It can range from a few sentences to a short essay. You can also have students draw and label important details of the object.

The neighborhood as the setting of a story

Just as sentence starters can help students get started writing, providing other story elements can have a similar effect. In this activity, the neighborhood is the setting for today's writing. This supplies some structure while allowing students to be creative.

Materials

- Paper and clipboard or notebook
- Pencil
- Optional: Read a book aloud featuring neighborhoods or streets as the setting before beginning this activity.

Read-aloud suggestions

- *Dream Street* by Tricia Elam Walker
- *Last Stop on Market Street* by Matt de la Peña
- *The Big Orange Splot* by Daniel Pinkwater
- *The Snowy Day* by Ezra Jack Keats
- *The Vanderbeekers of 141st Street* by Karina Yan Glaser (This is a chapter book – you may read a selection.)

Activity

Discuss setting and its importance in stories with your students. In some stories, the setting is central to the story itself, and in others, the setting is minor. If desired, read aloud an example of a story set in a neighborhood to the students. Explain that today they will write a story that takes place in the neighborhood around the school. Together venture out to choose a location for their stories and begin writing. (See Figure 3.17.)

A great writing style for this activity is a free write. A free write is an easy and relaxed writing method that helps students get their thoughts down without worrying about spelling, punctuation, or even if it makes sense. It is a great way to get reluctant writers writing! Later, students can work on the writing they generated during this activity by revising, editing, adding detail, and expanding on their ideas to improve the story.

Today is about taking one small idea (setting), spinning a story about it, and getting it down on paper. The only rule for free writes are that they begin writing and they do not stop the whole time. Usually, five to ten minutes is sufficient. You can set a timer and let everyone know to begin writing. If students are too far apart, have them estimate the

Figure 3.17 Students using the street as inspiration for writing stories
Source: Andrew Chiappetta

time or keep writing until they finish at least one side of the paper
(adjust to what works best for your students and situation).

To wrap up the activity, ask for volunteers to share their free writes with
a small group or as a whole group. Free writes are often funny when
read aloud because they are written very fast, are spontaneous, and
may have completely nonsensical parts. Therefore, they are a great
way for reluctant writers to feel comfortable sharing their work.

Adjusting the activity

Alternatively, students can write a few sentences and draw a picture.
They could also add to their story over several sessions.

Variation

Students can write several free writes over several neighborhood visits.
Then choose one story to revise and develop into a longer, more formal writing piece.

What is beyond that door?

This activity is inspired by the picture book *The Neighbors* by Einat Tsarfati. This book follows a curious girl who wonders and imagines what is behind the doors in her apartment building. For this activity, you will ask your students to pick a door in the neighborhood and imagine what could be behind it.

Materials

- *The Neighbors* by Einat Tsarfati
- Notebook
- Pencil

Activity

Begin by reading aloud the book *The Neighbors* by Einat Tsarfati to your class. After reading, ask if they have ever wondered what was behind a closed door. Explain that today the class will be visiting the neighborhood near the school. While there, they will choose a door and imagine what might be behind it (see Figure 3.18). Older students can write detailed descriptions. You can adjust this activity for beginning writers by having students draw a picture and add sentences describing what they think is behind the door.

NOTE Children are only looking and imagining what is behind the doors. This could be a good time to review safety rules about strangers. It is important that you evaluate the appropriateness of this activity based on your location and class needs.

Variations

- Have students revise and edit their work into final pieces. Compile the students' writing into a class book.
- Have each child or pair of students use the book *The Neighbors* by Einat Tsarfati as a mentor text. They can use the book as inspiration for writing their version of the story using doors from the neighborhood. This activity is especially popular with older students.

Nature riddles

Children love telling and guessing the answers to riddles! This activity allows children to write and share their riddles based on nature or

Figure 3.18 What will you find behind door number 100?
Source: Lina Kivaka / Pexels

observations of the neighborhood. Riddles are a fantastic task for reluctant writers because they are short and not overwhelming.

Materials

- Paper and clipboard or notebook
- A few example riddles and/or the book *So Imagine Me: Nature Riddles in Poetry* by Lynn Davies

Activity

Talk about what a riddle is and either read the example riddles and have students guess the answers or read the book *So Imagine Me: Nature Riddles in Poetry* by Lynn Davies aloud and have students guess the answers to each riddle. Discuss how riddles give just enough information in the clues for someone to guess without giving away the answer. Sometimes the clues included can have multiple meanings.

Explain that as they venture out into the neighborhood today, they will write their riddle about something in the neighborhood. It can be related to nature or the neighborhood itself. After students have written their riddle(s), divide them into groups and have them take turns sharing and guessing each other's riddles.

Example riddles

I am short and squat.
You rarely need me, but I am ready in an emergency.
What am I?
>   *Answer: A fire hydrant*

I am light gray.
I pick up after your snack.
I have two legs.
What am I?
>   *Answer: A pigeon*

Adjusting the activity

- Ask students to write more than one riddle.
- To work on reading skills, give students several teacher-created riddles using decodable text based on the neighborhood to solve while in the neighborhood. You can differentiate between reading levels by making separate sets of riddles for different groups.

Tourism agency

Children love to give tours and are eager to tell people why their town, neighborhood, or section of the world is unique. This project uses a variety of media formats as a way for students to show others why their neighborhood is special or highlight features that they think are important.

Materials

- Sample tourism brochures, audio tours, and commercials as models

Materials that may be needed depending on chosen project mediums

- Camera or device to take pictures
- Glue stick
- Paper

- Colored pencils
- Computer
- Printer
- Device to record sound and/or video

Activity

Explain to students that their task is to highlight the great things about their neighborhood and tell people why they should visit. This kind of project is often the job of a chamber of commerce or welcome center. They are often part of local government, and their job is to show people why their city, town, or area is a great place to visit.

This activity is best after completing several activities in the neighborhood, so they are familiar with its assets. You should plan at least two or three additional visits to the community for planning, research, writing, or filming. This project will typically require some indoor class time as well.

Have groups of students examine different types of ads for tourism. Have them evaluate them for effectiveness. What kind of information do they include? Have them briefly share their findings with the class.

Here are some ideas for projects that you can offer to your students. You can modify this list based on the resources available. Most of these options work best as group projects.

Project options

- Design a neighborhood walking tour. The final project can be written and/or an audio version.
- Writing a pamphlet or ad to encourage people to visit our neighborhood or town (see Figure 3.19).
- Write and film a commercial advertising the neighborhood or an aspect of it.
- Write a magazine or travel article about spending an afternoon in your neighborhood or review a park, shop, or other location of interest.
- Interview with a community member.

After groups have chosen a project format, have them brainstorm ideas and begin work on their project. Students working on walking tours

Figure 3.19 Example of pamphlet focusing on Ithaca, New York
Source: Rachel Tidd

or commercials will likely need an extended work period in the neighborhood to record/film.

Example project class schedule

Neighborhood visit #1: brainstorming and planning
Neighborhood visit #2: taking photos, filming, recording, writing
Neighborhood visit #3: finishing writing/filming
Classroom: finish writing, audio/video editing

After students have completed the project, have them present their work to their peers or a different class.

Adjusting the activity

- Provide a choice of only one or two types of projects if this type of work is new to your class.
- Provide templates or a list of items that must be included and/or a rubric to provide more structure and guidance for students to follow.

Outdoor Learning Tip: Utilizing Cemeteries and Graveyards

Cemeteries and graveyards are an often overlooked resource for outdoor learning! Older graveyards can be an excellent way to connect local history with general historical events. Dates on gravestones can provide opportunities to integrate math skills. Often cemeteries can provide needed green space in urban areas and can also be good places to seek out nature with your class. Consider getting parent permission before utilizing graveyards for learning, as some families may have cultural or other objections. (See Figure 3.21.)

Activity Ideas for Cemeteries

- **How old were they?** Integrate math by having students calculate how old people were when they died, how long ago they were buried, the person who lived the longest, and the oldest and newest headstones in the cemetery. This activity provides an opportunity for real-life applications of math skills.
- **Who is buried here?** Have students select and research a person on a gravestone. This works best in cemeteries with older gravestones. Consider asking local librarians and/or the local historical society to help your students research these past community members. Students can look in old newspapers for

Figure 3.21 Recording details from a gravestone
Source: Rachel Tidd

articles and obituaries, research where the person lived, and make connections about how historical events may have impacted their lives.

- **Gravestone rubbings:** Students can make rubbings of gravestones and research the period in which the person lived.
- **Phonics:** Have students look for and record examples of different phonics patterns in the names and other words on the gravestones. Give them a list of phonics patterns to search for.
- **Estimation:** Have groups estimate the number of people buried in the cemetery. What methods will they use? Compare estimates and see which group is the most accurate.
- **Timeline:** Have students choose ten gravestones and write names and the dates of which people passed away on index cards. Then have them arrange the cards to create a timeline. You can also have them use cards to add significant historical events to the timeline.
- **War and our community:** This activity is best for older students. Have students research the number of local people who served in different wars. They can calculate the total number of local people who served and the percentage of the local population it represented for various wars such as World War I. Additionally, they can compare how many people in their local community were directly involved in each war. They can make conclusions about which wars had the largest percentage of the local population directly serving, how that may have impacted the community, and/or which wars had the most significant impact on the local community.

Can you hear snow?

This activity is based on the book *Ten Ways to Hear Snow* by Cathy Camper. This book is a touching story about a young girl's relationship with her grandmother, who cannot see well. Walking to her grandmother's house she discovers all the many ways you can hear snow. After listening to the story students will write their own version of the story, such as ten ways to hear the rain, see wind, or another idea.

Materials

- *Ten Ways to Hear Snow* by Cathy Camper
- Notebook
- Pencil

Activity

Begin by reading the book *Ten Ways to Hear Snow* by Cathy Camper aloud to the class. Discuss the story and any personal connections they may have to it. Have they ever thought about ways you can tell something is there, even if it is quiet? As a class, brainstorm and record a list of other things that are quiet or silent but can be "heard" in other ways, like snow. You can also extend this to something you know is there even if you can't see it. Some examples are wind, rain, and sun.

After brainstorming, ask students to pick an item and write their version of "ten ways." Students may find it easier to work in pairs. Students can take their "ten ways" list and create a short book, adding illustrations.

Adjusting the activity

Have older students create their own "ten ways" picture book based on rain, wind, or another idea. This can be done individually or in pairs. Then arrange visits to younger classes for them to read their story aloud to the students.

Personification

The outdoor environment is the perfect place to introduce and apply the concept of personification. Personification is giving an object or idea human characteristics. Students will choose an item in the neighborhood to write sentences or a story using personification.

Materials

- Pencil
- Paper
- A picture book with examples of personification such as: *The Little Red Pen* by Janet Stevens and Susan Sevens Crummel, *The Little Engine That Could* by Watty Piper, *The Curious Garden* by Peter Brown, *Click, Clack, Moo: Cows That Type* by Doreen Cronin, and *Sweet Tooth* by Margie Palatini

Activity

Introduce or review the idea of personification and give examples. Then read and discuss with your class the book that features personification. The use of personification is very common in picture books and students are often surprised how they never really noticed it before! Many of your students may already be familiar with the book titles listed, but they will be surprised how looking at the stories through this new lens reveals a new dimension to the story.

After reading, take a walk in an area of the neighborhood. Have students spread out and choose an object to personify in their writing. Beginning writers may write a sentence or two and add an illustration, while older students can write a short paragraph or story.

Neighborhood odes

Gary Soto is a Mexican American author who writes books, poems, and short stories focusing on Mexican American or Chicano culture and characters. He often incorporates Spanish words into his writing. This book of odes uses descriptive language to highlight the significance of seemingly ordinary objects. This activity will encourage children to think and write creatively about the items and places in their neighborhood!

Materials

- Paper and clipboard or notebook
- *Neighborhood Odes: A Poetry Collection* by Gary Soto
- Copies of a poem for each student or pair of students
- Chart paper or another method to record student answers
- Pencil

Activity

Read a few of Gary Soto's odes aloud to your students. Together discuss why they think Gary Soto chose these objects to write an ode about. How does he feel about these items? How can they tell? (Ask them to give examples.)

Give each student or pair of students a copy of one of the odes. Have them examine the ode for descriptive words, metaphors, repeating words, and words in a different language. Do the lines rhyme? Are there stanzas? How does the author's word choice affect the meaning, tone, or imagery of the ode?

After students have had time to read and analyze the ode, lead a discussion about what they found. Make a list of student responses to refer to later.

After they have shared, explain that today they will be writing their own ode about something they like, enjoy, or feel is important in the neighborhood around the school. The class will visit the neighborhood together and have time to choose and write an ode featuring their selected object, place, or person. Odes can come in many different forms. Their ode can be similar in style and structure to Gary Soto's ode or their own creation. Allow time for writing the odes outdoors. (See Figure 3.20.)

If time allows, ask for volunteers to share their odes with the class. Students can revise and edit their odes into more polished pieces later in the classroom if desired.

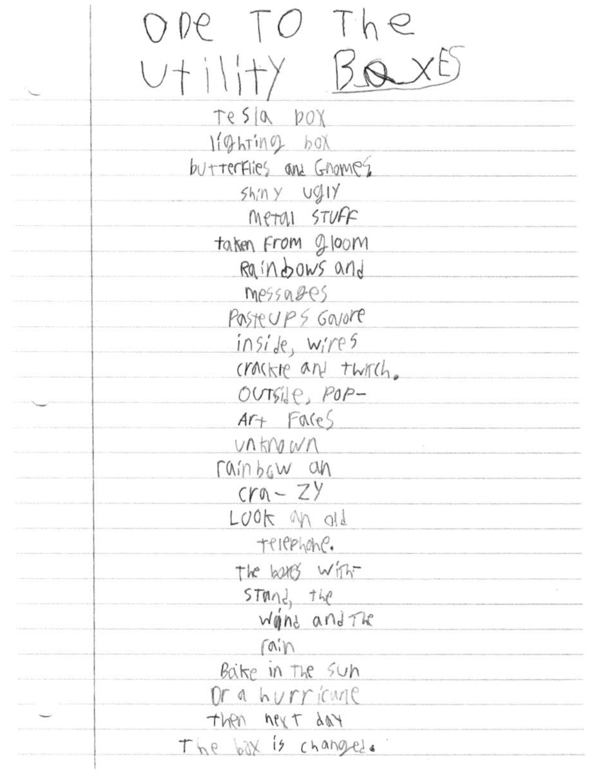

ODE TO THE
UTILITY BOXES

Tesla box
lighting box
butterflies and Gnomes
shiny ugly
metal stuff
taken from gloom
rainbows and
messages
PasteUPS Galore
inside, wires
crackle and twitch.
Outside, Pop-
Art Faces
unknown
rainbow an
cra-zy
Look an old
telephone.
The boxs with
stand, the
wind and the
rain
Bake in the sun
Or a hurricane
then next day
The box is changed.

Figure 3.20 Student work sample: An Ode to Painted Utility Boxes
Source: Rachel Tidd

Adjusting the activity

- Try using a simpler poem style such as acrostic, or haiku for beginning writers.
- If the odes are too difficult for students to read independently, read a few odes aloud and analyze them together.

Extensions

- **Using words to show importance:** Have students write another ode about something important to them. How can they use words to convey this to the reader? How did Gary Soto use words to show the reader why the objects he chose were important?
- **Reading odes by other authors:** Extend the study of odes by learning about Pablo Neruda's poetry. Older students may enjoy reading *Ode to*

an Onion and *Ode to My Socks* by Pablo Neruda or *Ode to Kool-Aid* by Marcus Jackson, both of which are easily found online. Younger students may enjoy hearing the picture book adaptation *Ode to an Onion: Pablo Neruda and His Muse* by Alexandria Giardino, or *Crown: an Ode to the Fresh Cut* by Derrick Barnes.

Final Thoughts

In this chapter, you learned how to use the features around your school to enhance your lessons. You learned how to use environmental print to support reading skills, how to look for arrays around the neighborhood, and even how to use street trees in a yearlong study! In the next chapter, we go farther afield to explore parks and other natural areas for a more immersive learning experience in nature.

04 Exploring Farther Afield

Taking your class to parks or natural areas farther away from the school provides a more immersive experience in nature. There is often a greater diversity of plants, animals, and habitats. While these field trips usually take more planning, they are often among the children's favorite activities!

The Plants and Animals Around Us

Many children do not have much background knowledge about their habitats in their local area. Getting out and visiting new places gives students a chance to learn more about the plants and animals in their local area. Activities in this section help children practice essential academic skills while gaining a deeper knowledge of the plant and animal world.

Math activities

Math can be found everywhere, even in the most natural habitats. These activities will help students see how math can be found in flowers and leaves and when doing activities such as sledding races!

Flower geometry

Flowers are a fantastic example of how geometry and nature are intertwined. When you look closely at flowers, geometric shapes and patterns reveal themselves. Observing these patterns in the natural environment can be an excellent way to link geometry skills with real-life examples. Students are often amazed at how many shapes and patterns they find in nature when they begin looking!

Materials

- Paper or notebook
- Pencil
- Optional: camera or tablet capable of taking pictures to examine later

Expanding Studies Beyond Natural Areas

While this chapter's focus is mainly on activities in natural areas, meaningful outdoor learning experiences are not limited to only natural areas and parks. The teachers at the PS 146 – The Brooklyn New School in New York City did an extensive unit study of bridges, visiting several different kinds including the Brooklyn Bridge (see Figure 4.1). PS 290 –The Manhattan New School studies different neighborhoods such as Harlem and Chinatown, visiting each one (and tasting the foods!). Other schools have examined the different types of food production from community gardens to large-scale farms. Consider studying important features of the areas near your school such as subway stations, geographic features of your region, unique neighborhoods, large city parks (many classes in New York City study Central Park and visit multiple times over their study), the water system in the city, types of farms or ranches, monuments, and architectural styles or tall buildings. The possibilities for outdoor learning are endless!

Figure 4.1 Students from The Brooklyn New School visit the Brooklyn Bridge for their study of bridges
Source: Andrew Chiappetta

Begin by showing examples of flowers that form geometric shapes. These shapes can be observed by looking at the shape created by the outside edges of the flowers. For example, flowers with five petals make a pentagon shape around the outside of the petals, and a five-pointed star can be made by connecting the petals (see Figures 4.2, 4.3, and 4.4).

Have them sketch the flowers and the geometric shapes they discover in their notebook or on paper. They should label their drawings with the geometric shape(s) and the flower species. Students may want to investigate the number of shapes they can find in flowers or which shapes are most common.

Collect 100

It is through the process of performing this activity that learning and mathematical thinking happen! Collecting 100 natural items sounds deceptively simple, but it requires students to devise a plan, organize, recount, group, and keep track of the items they have and how many

Figure 4.2 The petals of a daffodil form a hexagon
Source: Rachel Tidd

Figure 4.3 Examples of triangles observed on a tulip
Source: Rachel Tidd

Figure 4.4 The petals of a wild strawberry flower form a pentagon
Source: Rachel Tidd

more they need (see Figure 4.5). Another layer of complexity is added to this task when working in pairs or small groups. This activity also builds number sense by building an understanding of the quantity of 100.

Materials

- Area to collect natural materials
- A way to keep track of items found such as ten frames drawn in the sand/dirt or chalk
- A large 100 chart (fabric, laminated, or drawn) or simply rows of ten items each

Activity

The amount of structure and support you provide your students for this activity will vary based on the needs of your students. For students who need more support, provide more direction on how to keep track of the

Figure 4.5 Using a giant 100 chart to collect 100 nature items
Source: Elizabeth Snyder

items they are collecting. For example, you may suggest they draw ten frames, make piles or rows of ten, or use a 100 chart (see Figures 4.6 and 4.7). For more advanced students, you may simply ask them to collect 100 items and leave the organization and planning up to them!

Lead a short discussion once everyone is finished with the activity. What strategies did students or groups use to keep track of the materials as they collected items? Was this activity more difficult or easier than they initially thought? How many items did the class collect altogether?

Variations

Have groups or even the entire class collect a much larger number such as 500 or even 1,000. Doing a number this size is best done in a group as it is more time-consuming. However, collecting the larger number helps students conceptualize the difference in magnitude between 100 and 1,000!

Figure 4.6 Collecting 100 rocks using a 100 chart
Source: Alyssa Conley

Outdoor Learning Tip: Stick Safety

Children are naturally attracted to sticks. They are an amazing material that provides endless open-ended play and learning opportunities! Students can safely use sticks outdoors! Discuss stick safety with your class. Demonstrate how you must be aware of the space around you when playing with a stick. This is particularly true if playing with a large stick. Show examples of proper and improper spacing between peers when playing with sticks and ask students to brainstorm some guidelines for stick play at school. An excellent book to read about sticks is *Not a Stick* by Antoinette Portis.

Figure 4.7 Collecting and counting black walnuts for the collect 100 activity
Source: Christal Gamble

Skip counting and multiplication using flowers and leaves

Flower petals and leaves are a fantastic way to model and practice skip counting and multiplication. This is a great way to show examples of math in the natural world. Petals, leaves, and pine needles all grow in groups. For example, wild strawberry petals, violets, white pine needles, and apple blossoms have five petals, clover leaves grow in threes, many maple leaves have three points, and many types of daffodils have six outer petals (see Figure 4.8). This activity can also be done in parks, community gardens, or streets with plantings and landscaping.

Figure 4.8 Students observing groups of daffodils for multiplication practice

Source: Andrew Chiappetta

Materials

- Location with a variety of trees, flowers, plants
- Plant field guides
- Notebook or paper
- Pencil
- Additional materials for specific activities

Activities

Make a pressed flower fact book: Choose a multiplication fact family. Collect flowers, leaves, or needles and glue or tape on the page to visually model a math fact. For example, two sets of clover leaves (grow in threes) show the multiplication fact 2×3. Ask students to make one page for each fact up to 10 or 12 and include the fact and answer. Pressing the leaves or flowers between pages in a large book, between layers of newspaper with a heavy book on top, can make the plants stay flat. This makes them easier to glue or tape into a book. This activity can be differentiated by showcasing addition facts or counting.

Nature journaling and multiples: Integrate math into nature journaling by having students find and record multiples and/or skip counting by using examples of flowers and plants for each number. When students find an example for a number, they draw the flower or leaves 10 times in their journals. Then label each flower with the multiple and/or the multiplication fact (see Figure 4.9). Challenge them to find as many examples as possible or an example of each of the numbers 1–10.

Finding groups: Find and observe groups or collect several flowers with a set number of petals. Ask students to find the total number of petals by adding, skip counting, or using multiplication to find the total number of petals. Have them record their calculations in their notebooks. You can also do this activity using leaves and pine needles that grow in groups or by counting the lobes or points of leaves such as maple and oak and bunches of five needles on the white pine tree (see Figure 4.10).

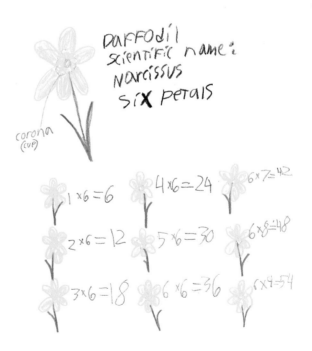

Figure 4.9 **Example of writing multiplication fact families using daffodils**
Source: Rachel Tidd

Figure 4.10 Using the points on leaves to practice skip counting by threes
Source: Rachel Tidd

Calendar of bloom

Have you ever noticed that you can tell what time of year it is by what is blooming? Where I live the first daffodils and dandelions announce spring, the chicory and daisies welcome summer, and the deep mustard yellow goldenrods and purple asters put on a show for fall. By tuning into these changes and recording which flowers are in bloom on a calendar, students will start making connections between the month, what is blooming, and the seasonal cycles of the year.

Materials

- Copies of a blank calendar
- Pencil
- Colored pencils
- Areas with flowers to observe

Activity

This ongoing project tracks when flowers bloom throughout the year. Students will record which flowers are blooming over time, looking for trends and making connections between the current season and past seasons they have experienced.

Begin by taking a class walk and noticing what is in bloom now. Model for students how to fill out the calendar for the current month/year if the calendar is blank. They should add numbers and label the days of the week and the year. Then show them how to record the flowers in the day's square on the calendar. Ask them to draw a picture of the flower and write the name of one or more species of flowers blooming (see Figure 4.11).

As the school year progresses, continue taking a weekly or biweekly class walk to observe any new species of flowers that are blooming and record them on their calendar. Over time, they will be able to see how different flowers bloom at other times. You may wish to pause periodically so they can examine their observations and discuss them as a class. One pattern students may notice is that the colors of flowers are similar during the same time of year. Think of all the golden hues in the fall, for example. And white flowers in spring!

Variations

• **Color-coded calendar:** You can also simply write the species name in the box and color the square the primary color of the flower. To see

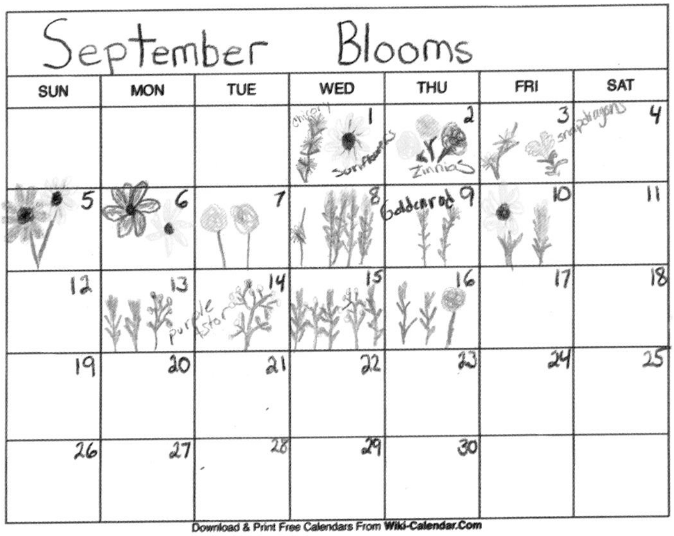

Figure 4.11 An example calendar of bloom
Source: Rachel Tidd

color patterns more easily, students may wish to color the whole week, reflecting on the most common or prominent color observed.

- **Class calendar:** Add this information to your class calendar or make a class calendar of bloom for display.
- **Make predictions:** Have children predict what will be the next flower to bloom!
- **Nature journal:** Ask students to write a nature journal entry detailing all the flowers they saw and add illustrations for each walk.
- **Research:** Have students research the flowers they observe. Are they native, invasive, or planted? What is the history of the plant? Special features? Where does it grow well? Is it common or rare? Does it grow in your area normally or was it planted?
- **Watercolor art:** Take watercolors outside and have students paint and re-create the colors they see! Then label each color with the flower name or a new name they create.
- **More data:** To collect more data, consider sending the calendar of bloom home with students to record the flowers they see during a specified month.

Sledding races

This activity is always a hit with students! Integrating math, graphing, and science concepts into sledding make for a fun and educational afternoon outside.

If your school does not have sleds, you may want to ask families if they have sleds that the class could borrow for this activity. Another potential option is to have students design their sleds in a separate STEAM project. Consider other items such as hard plastic lunch trays or cookie sheets that might make interesting "sleds." It can be fun to try different items and see which works best and is the fastest! If you do not have snow where you live, consider sack, scooter, or toy car races.

Materials

- Stopwatches for each group
- A hill or snow pile created by a plow to sled down
- Sleds (store-bought or DIY)
- Sticks or another object to mark the run distance
- Measuring tape
- Notebook or laminated paper
- Writing utensil appropriate for the method of recording

Before planning to do this activity with your class, scope out a suitable location with a hill. Large piles of snow created when plowing can also work as an alternative location if a suitable hill is difficult to find. Always evaluate the area for potential hazards such as trees, roads, and large objects.

Introduce and explain to your class that today they will be experimenting with sleds to see how fast they can make them travel down the hill. If using a stopwatch is new for your students, give a brief explanation of how to use them.

Have students measure and mark off their sledding track by marking the start and the finish with a stick. These reference sticks will ensure each run is the same distance and helps the students time runs consistently. They should measure and record the distance between the two sticks.

Groups should sled down the hill a few times to pack down the snow before collecting data. Have each group member take a turn going down the hill to ensure fairness. Have them check to ensure their sled travels past the reference stick placed at the bottom of the hill. Adjust the location of the reference stick if necessary.

Have students take turns going down the hill and recording how long it takes for them to travel from the top stick to the bottom stick. They should start the timer when the tip of the sled passes the top stick and then stop the timer when the tip of the sled reaches the stick at the bottom of the hill. In addition, they should record the name of the rider.

After everyone has had a turn, experiment with the number of passengers, passenger position, and type of sled to see which combination is fastest. They should record the data and specific combinations for each run.

Encourage students to actively interpret their data after each run and adjust their trial combinations if desired. Questions they may wish to consider might be: Which sled run was the fastest so far? Why do you think it was the fastest? Are the individual passenger runs getting faster as time goes on? Why do you believe that was happening? They can apply the knowledge gained from their data to try new combinations of passengers and other alterations in real time to help them make the sled runs faster! (See Figure 4.12.)

Graphing, calculating, and analyzing the data can be done on-site or when back inside the classroom, particularly if you want students to graph their results on paper. To graph their results outside, laminate graph paper so it is waterproof and use dry-erase crayons or colored pencils for recording.

Ask each group to compile their data and create a graph showing the run times. They can then calculate the group average, the fastest (shortest time) and slowest (longest time) run, the mode, and the median run time for their group. If the distance/runs of the groups were similar, you may choose to compile the data, make a graph, and calculate the statistics as a whole class.

Have students interpret the data and discuss/answer questions such as:

- What was the fastest run?
- Why do you think it went the fastest?
- What factors seemed to impact the time/speed it took for a sled to travel down the run?

Figure 4.12 A sledding experiment using a giant snowball
    as the load
    Source: Rachel Tidd

- Based on today's experience, what would you do differently if you went back to sled more and why?
- Did you notice anything else about the data?
- How do you think changing the hill's incline would impact the sled's speed? Explain.
- Compare your data with other groups or with the class data. How is it different? How is it similar? Discuss and formulate some possible reasons that the data was similar or different.

Students in upper grades can calculate the sled's speed and graph the data. The equation for speed = distance/time.

Measuring snow people

Children of all ages enjoy building snow people and snow creatures! Put a mathematical twist on this classic activity by having children measure the height, width, and circumference. Advanced students can calculate the volume of each section and/or the whole creation. Extend this activity by having students write a story using their snow creation as the main character in their story. If you do not have snow in your location, try using sand or other natural materials.

Materials

- Packable snow (or sand, clay, or other materials)
- Measuring tape for each group of students
- Laminated paper
- Dry-erase crayons or colored pencils
- Natural materials for decorating
- Book about snow people to read aloud

Suggestions for books about snow people:

- *The Biggest Snowman Ever* by Steven Kroll
- *The Biggest, Best Snowman* by Margery Cuyler
- *Snowzilla* by Janet Lawler
- *Making a Friend* by Tammi Sauer
- *All You Need for a Snowman* by Alice Schertle
- *Making a Friend* by Alison McGhee

Activity

Set the stage for this fun activity by reading a book about building snow people, such as *Snowzilla* by Janet Lawler. Then explain that today they will work together to build their snow person or snow creature and measure them (see Figure 4.13). Review the metrics you want them to measure or calculate for their creature when they have finished building. You can have students measure each ball's height, width, and circumference and record the numbers on their laminated paper. Divide the class into groups and have them spread out and begin creating their snow people.

To make a traditional snow creature out of giant balls of snow, students should start by making a ball of snow approximately 6–12 inches in diameter. Next, roll the ball in the snow. As the ball rolls, it picks up a layer of snow and grows larger. Keep rolling until the ball is the desired size (see Figure 4.14).

When finished building their snow creation, they can measure and calculate its height, length, and circumference. After completing

Figure 4.13 A snow cat
Source: Rachel Tidd

Figure 4.14 Building a giant snow person
Source: Rachel Tidd

their measurements and/or calculations, they may add details to their creations using natural materials that they find nearby.

Adjusting the activity

Upper grade students can calculate the volume of each sphere and the total volume of the creation.

Extensions

- Have students write a story about their snow person or creature as the main character.
- Have students write a how-to that describes how to make a snow person or creature.

Variation

- Have students compete to make the largest snowball, tallest creation, or the most creatively decorated snowperson, creature, or cake (see Figure 4.15). Then have them write a story about or including their creation.

Outdoor Learning Tip: Warm Drinks

When outside in cold weather for long periods, a warm drink in a thermos can help make you feel warmer and keeps kids happy outside! Herbal teas and lower-sugar hot cocoa are kid favorites, but even just warm water is helpful. Ask students to bring a thermos or insulated water bottle with a hot drink. You can also get a few large thermoses or carafes to provide hot beverages to your students (see Figure 4.16).

Figure 4.15 Building and decorating a snow cake is a fun
alternative to snow creatures
Source: Rachel Tidd

Reading and writing activities

A range of exciting activities to engage children in reading and writing can be found farther afield! These activities utilize these environments' diverse experiences and natural resources to practice and teach essential literacy skills.

Collect the alphabet

While an alphabet activity may sound like something for younger students, this activity can be quite challenging for all ages! Finding a natural

Figure 4.16 Warm drinks can help keep you warm in
cold weather
Source: Rachel Tidd

item or plant to represent each letter of the alphabet requires knowledge
of the natural world, creative thinking, phonemic awareness, and more!

Materials

- A grid with a space for each letter of the alphabet drawn with chalk on
  a paved surface, on a large piece of paper, or on fabric with a
  permanent marker (make sure there is space for each letter)
- Pencil or chalk
- Area to collect natural items
- Flower, tree, and weed field guides for more difficult variations

Activity

The most basic form of this activity involves groups of students working
together to collect a natural item representing each letter the alphabet. You can specify that the item found begins with the sound (or one
of the sounds) that the letter can make, the spelling of the item begins
with the letter, or both. Draw a large grid on a hard surface, fabric,
or on a piece of paper. Using a large grid allows students to place

the item in the square representing the letter. Alternatively, you can provide each student with a piece of paper with boxes for each letter. Students can record the name of each item or sketch a picture of it in the appropriate box.

Finding an item representing all the letters can be quite challenging. Some letters will take creativity to find something that represents them (see Figure 4.17). Finding something for every letter may not be possible depending on the time of year and location. You can have groups compete against each other to see who can find the most items!

Variations

- Define a category from which the items must come, such as trees, plants, and flower species. This will likely require students to use field guides to identify plants. This is an excellent way for students to learn more species of plants! They also can pool their knowledge as a group to identify plant species and find more letters.

Figure 4.17 Natural items collected by students and placed on the letter sound that they begin with
Source: Rachel Tidd

Similes and metaphors

Using nature and natural elements is a fantastic way to learn about and practice writing similes and metaphors. Writing on leaves with a permanent marker provides novelty and the temporary nature of the material often appeals to reluctant writers.

Materials

- Leaves or paper on which to write similes and metaphors
- Permanent marker or pencil
- Example similes and/or metaphors to share with your class

Activity

Similes compare two things using the words *like* or *as*. For example, *the trees branches sheltered the creatures below like an umbrella*. We use a metaphor as a comparison that refers to a person, place, or thing as being something else. This type of comparison does not use the words *like* or *as*. For example, *an apple is nature's candy*. Share a few examples of similes and metaphors with your class and discuss the differences. If similes and metaphors are new to your students, focus on one type at a time and extend this activity to two days.

Then have them venture out to write an example of a simile and a metaphor inspired by the natural environment. They can use a permanent marker to write the similes and metaphors on leaves or use a pencil and record their work on paper. Have them share their writing in groups or with the whole class.

Variations

- Have students select one of their similes or metaphors and write it on paper. Then they can add an illustration. Collect and bind all the papers into a class nature simile and metaphor book.
- Have students write similes and/or metaphors about different categories such as plants, animals, houses, buildings, etc.

Creating a wild seed catalog

Each spring, gardeners look forward to receiving seed catalogs in the mail and planning out their gardens. In this activity, students will collect different seeds and create their own seed catalogs.

Materials

- Examples of seed catalogs
- Paper

- Stapler
- Collected seeds or time and location to collect seeds
- Plant field guides
- Container to collect seeds in, such as an empty egg carton

NOTE You can order free seed catalogs online from seed companies. You can also ask if any of your students' families have any catalogs they could donate. Digital versions of seed catalogs are also readily available from many seed companies and can be printed for this activity. One company that has lovely seed catalogs in digital form is seedsavers.org.

Activity

Have students look at examples of seed catalogs and discuss how the companies describe the seeds, the plant that grows from the seed, how they use pictures, and other information included on the page. Explain that today they will work in groups designing and writing their seed catalog for the seeds they collected.

Have groups of students look for and collect samples of seeds. For this activity, it is important to know what plant the seed came from. Students may use field guides or the internet to assist in identifying any seeds they are unsure of. After they have collected and identified several different seeds, have them each select one seed and design a page of a seed catalog showcasing the seed(s). Their page should include the plant's name, drawing, a description, and a price.

Have students assemble everyone's finished pages into a book. Add a blank paper for the cover. Choose a title for their seed catalog as a group and illustrate the cover.

Variations

- You can also make a class seed catalog instead of group seed catalogs by having each child choose a different kind of seed and create their catalog page. To do it this way you will need to make sure that there is a different seed specimen for each student in your class. Depending on your geographic location, class size, biodiversity of the area, and season, this may not be possible.
- Instead of a catalog, you may wish to have students design a seed packet. For this, you will need some example seed packets and small

envelopes. They can place the seeds inside the envelopes, illustrate the front, and write important information on the back of the envelope.

- For beginning writers or those who need more support, create a simple outline of the page layout.

Tracks tell a story

This activity encourages children not only to identify animal tracks but also to consider the story behind the tracks. Using critical thinking skills and inferences, children can construct either a realistic or a fantastical tale based on the tracks!

Materials

- Paper or notebook
- Pencil
- Access to an area to find tracks of animals (squirrels, dogs, and cats work fine!)
- Animal track field guide
- Optional: camera

Activity

Have groups venture out and look for animal tracks. Flat muddy areas near streams, ponds, or lakes are excellent locations to look for tracks because many kinds of animals are drawn to water. Looking for tracks on trails after it rains can also be a good strategy. When students find animal prints, have them look carefully at where the tracks are located and the plants and land features nearby and record these details (see Figure 4.18).

Questions to consider when observing tracks:

- What direction was the animal going?
- What direction did the animal come from?
- Does it look like the animal was moving fast or slow?
- Are there any clues as to what the animal was doing? Passing through, browsing for food (deer/rabbits), getting water, or hunting?

If students do not know what type of animal made the tracks, have them use a field guide to identify the animal. You may wish to have them take a picture of the tracks and the area if you do not plan to complete the writing assignment at the location.

Figure 4.18 Observing animal tracks found in a creek bed
Source: Rachel Tidd

Once groups have found and identified their tracks, discuss with students how animal tracks are evidence of animals and their movement. By looking closely at the clues, we can construct a possible story of what the animal may have been doing. A great way to record relevant information about the animal tracks is by answering the five W questions: Who? What? Where? When? And why?

Have groups work together to answer the questions and create a possible story behind the animal tracks. Then have each student work on writing a story that explains the background behind the animal tracks. The story can be realistic or fantasy. The only requirement is to include the facts they gathered about the tracks today.

Adjusting the activity

• Differentiate this activity for the lower grades by having children only work on answering the five W questions.

- Provide a simple graphic organizer to help them organize their answers to the five W questions and their story writing.

Extension

Pair this with the track casting activity in the science section.

Write from a leaf's perspective

This writing activity can help students understand perspective and its role in how stories are told.

Materials

- Paper
- Pencil
- Colored pencils

In this activity, have students imagine what it would be like to be a leaf. Then they will make up a story that describes the leaf's perspective and tell it to you. Perspective is the lens through which someone sees the world or from which the story is told. Every person or character's perspective is unique. Often students mix perspective up with the point of view, which is who is narrating or telling the story (first, second, or third person).

Questions to inspire

- What would it feel like to suddenly drop from a tree that had been your only home?
- What might it be like to experience a thunderstorm as a leaf?

Short Example Story

I had hung on this branch all summer. I loved being tossed by the wind and feeling the warm sun. Every day was beautiful.

Recently, however, I started noticing some strange things. I noticed that the nights were getting a bit chilly. Was it my imagination or were the days getting shorter? To top it all off, my lovely dark green color was turning orange! What was happening?!

Then suddenly, a strong gust of wind blew through the forest. It was then that I felt my stem lift from the branch! The wind instantly took me. I was twirling and swirling in the currents. I was terrified!

- What kinds of things might happen to a leaf? (bugs eating it, changing color in the fall, getting a fungus)

Have students write their stories and share in groups or ask for volunteers to share with the whole class. You can choose to have students further revise and edit their stories over the next few days or simply use this as a quick, informal writing assignment. Specify the length and expectations appropriate for your student's grade and writing levels before students begin writing.

Build a setting

Building a miniature house or village using natural materials inspires children's creativity. We can then build on this hands-on activity by having students write a story inspired by their creations.

Materials

- Natural materials
- Paper
- Pencil
- Optional: a camera or tablet to take photos of their creations

Activity

For this activity, have students find a spot to build a house, or other structure using natural materials they collect nearby (see Figure 4.19). Students can work on the construction individually, in pairs, or groups. After they have finished building their structures, have students imagine a story that takes place in the building/s that they created. Often students like to imagine these small structures as housing magical creatures such as fairies or gnomes, but anything goes! (See Figure 4.20.)

To help students generate ideas, you may want to pose questions such as:

- Who lives here?
- What do they do here?
- Why are they here? Did they choose to be here or are they here for another reason?
- What is a problem that they might face?

Use a generic graphic organizer to help children brainstorm vital elements of their story such as the characters, problem, and solution. If you want students to add to their writing at a later time, have them

Figure 4.19 Students love to build miniature houses and write about who lives there
Source: Rachel Tidd

Figure 4.20 A cozy fairy house
Source: Rachel Tidd

take a photo of their creations. When finished, students may share their stories with the class or in smaller groups.

To practice expository writing skills, students can write a "how-to" on the process of building a small house using natural materials.

Science

Seeing habitats and the plants and animals that live there firsthand is the best way to learn life science! The following section uses the resources found in most natural areas to learn about plants, birds, and insects.

Plant classification with a dichotomous key

Classification is an important concept in both math and science. Dichotomous keys are often used to identify plants. Often these types of keys can be found in field guides. In this activity, students learn about classification by creating a simple dichotomous key for classification based on the features of plants that they have collected.

Materials

- Collected samples of plants such as leaves or flowers
- Large sheet of paper
- Glue/tape
- Pencil
- Marker
- Field guide with an example of a dichotomous key or copies of a dichotomous key

Activity

To begin, give examples and explain how a dichotomous key works (see Figure 4.21). Then ask pairs or groups of students to collect 8–10 different samples of plants such as flowers or leaves. They should decide what to call their collection as a whole. This is their starting point. In the following example, all the samples were leaves. This became the starting point for their dichotomous key. Other options could be "plants found in Smith Park" or "flowers in a meadow." Whatever they choose to call their main category, they should write it on the top of their paper.
You may wish to model the process for students or lead the class through each step of the activity.

Figure 4.21 Example of a simple dichotomous key

Once students have collected their plant samples, and chosen a category, they sort the plants they gathered into two main categories according to a single characteristic. The characteristic could be shape, plant parts (leaves, flowers, stem), texture, color, etc. The characteristic should be something physical that can be observed. In the example key, the first two categories are pointy leaves and rounded leaves. Have them label and draw arrows from the main category to two new categories. Be sure to leave space to glue or tape an example specimen for each category onto the paper.

Next, have them examine the plants in each new category and decide on what feature of the plants they should sort by. In the example, we further sorted the rounded leaves category into leaves with lobes and those without lobes. Have them draw arrows and label the two new categories on the paper. There should be a total of four new categories in this step. As before, make sure they leave room to glue or tape a plant specimen under or next to each category names.

Stop here or repeat the process until only one plant remains in each category. Then have students choose examples for each category and glue or tape the plant samples next to each category label (see Figure 4.22).

Figure 4.22 Example of a dichotomous key made by a student
Source: Rachel Tidd

Variations

- Have students use a field guide or official dichotomous key to identify and label each plant at the end step of their dichotomous key.
- Focus on one category such as leaves or flowers to create a dichotomous key that helps people identify the type of tree or plant.
- Have students use a dichotomous key to identify trees or plants in the local area. How is this kind of key useful? What are the similarities and differences between the keys that they made?

How seeds spread scavenger hunt

The wide range of methods plants have evolved to spread their seeds is fascinating. Students will look for examples of how seeds spread in this scavenger hunt.

Materials

- Container to collect seeds
- Clear tape
- Pencil
- Clipboard
- *How Seeds Spread* worksheet or paper for recording (worksheet can be found at discoverwildlearning.com/wild-learning-book-resources)

- Book about how seeds travel such as *Flip, Float, Fly: Seeds on the Move* by JoAnn Early Macken, *Seeds Move* by Robin Page, or *A Seed Is Sleepy* by Dianna Aston.

Introduce and discuss how seeds can spread or travel by reading a book about seeds and how they travel before the activity. Together with students, make a list of the main ways seeds spread. The most common categories are wind, water, animal scat, attached or carried by animals, and gravity. Some seeds are spread after fire or explosion.

Have students work in pairs to find an example of a seed for each method that plants use to spread seeds. Have students use the worksheet or divide their paper into boxes and label (5–6) boxes with one way that seeds can spread (wind, water, animal scat, attached to or carried by animals, gravity, and optional fire or explosion). When they find an example seed, they can tape or sketch the seed in the box that corresponds to how they are spread. If they know what plant the seed is from, have them label it! If they are unsure, provide field guides to help them identify them.

Afterward, have students share some of the seeds they found and how they spread with the whole class. Some questions you may wish to discuss together might be, what is the most common way that seeds are spread based on their findings? Do some seeds spread in more than one way? Which category do you think is the most successful for spreading seeds? Why?

Variations

- Have students find five different seeds and record the methods that they spread. They can draw or tape the seeds into their notebooks and add labels.
- Have students collect and graph data showing how many plants use each distribution method.

Insect inventory

The insect world is vast and often is mostly invisible to us. Having students look for insects in a specified area and creating graphs of the results will help children understand this important group of living things.

Materials

- Location to look for insects
- Paper
- Graph paper
- Pencil
- String
- Sticks
- Insect field guides that cover your geographic area

Activity

Before embarking on the insect activity, ensure that the students understand what an insect is. Key physical features of insects are a head, thorax, abdomen, and six legs. They also have an exoskeleton. Review guidelines on interacting respectfully with insects and other living things.

Divide the class into groups and give them each a 24-foot piece of string. They will use this string to mark off a square- or rectangle-shaped area for their insect inventory. Once they have laid the string on the ground in the area they want to inventory, they can use small sticks to hold each of the four corners of the rectangle and tie the two ends of the string together (see Figure 4.23).

Have the students start at one end of the square, identifying and recording the insects found. They should list each species they find and add tallies when they find more of the same species. Students can use field guides to look up unfamiliar species. They should keep cataloging the number and species of insects until they have finished looking through the entire area.

When they have finished their inventory, they should create a graph using graph paper to show their data. Scientists often must present their data in graphs to help people understand their findings.

Adjusting the activity

- Use a tally chart or graph of only a few of the species found.
- Have students write a paragraph explaining their findings or an entire lab report.
- Posters can also be a great way to display graphs and findings.

Figure 4.23 Conducting an insect inventory
Source: Rachel Tidd

Variations

This type of inventory is often called a bio blitz. For variety, you can have students search for plants or other categories such as fungus, lichen, birds, etc.

Bird talk

Students delight in being able to interpret bird language! Once they listen closely to birds and learn a few key attributes of bird communication, it opens up a new awareness of the natural world.

Materials

- The book *Bird Talk* by Ann Jonas
- Paper
- Pencil

Learn More About How Birds Communicate

Additional information about bird language can be found in the children's book *Bird Talk: What Birds Are Saying and Why* by Lita Judge. For adults and older students who would like to increase their understanding of bird communication, the book *What the Robin Knows: How Birds Reveal the Secrets of the Natural World* by Jon Young is excellent.

Additional Bird Language Resources

An Educator's Guide to the Language of Birds by Rebecca Coulter https://www.sbnature.org/uploads/pages/BirdLanguage-1523472660.pdf

The Backyard Birdsong Guide by Donald Kroodsma is an excellent series of books produced by the Cornell Lab of Ornithology that have outstanding recordings of bird calls right in the book. There are several in the series covering North America.

- Access to a location with a variety of birds
- If your students are new to bird calls, you may want to prepare some audio clip examples of the five categories of bird language

Activity

In this activity, children will listen to birds and record their sounds using phonetic spelling. Introduce the activity by reading the book *Bird Talk* by Ann Jonas. After reading, discuss how birds have a language of their own and pose the following questions to the class:

- How do birds sound when there is a predator nearby?
- How do they sound when they are happy and greeting the day?
- What other sounds do they make?

After the discussion, introduce the five main categories of bird language.

- Song
- Alarm
- Aggression
- Companionship/mating
- Juvenile begging

Talk about each category and give (or have students come up with) examples of each type. If bird language is very new for your students, you may want to prepare some audio samples ahead of time to give more concrete examples.

Next, explain that today they will listen to birds and write the sounds they hear on paper. They can use letters and words to represent the sounds they hear birds make in their notebooks. If they know what bird species made the sound or what category the sound falls in, they can also record that information. Remind students to stay quiet and try not to move around too much so that they hear as many birds as possible.

After the observation time is finished, bring the class together to discuss what they saw and heard. You may wish to record their observations on chart paper using columns for each category of bird language.

Suggested discussion questions include:

- What kind of sounds did the birds make?
- What category were the sounds in?
- What do you think they were trying to communicate?
- What types of birds were making them? (They can describe the bird if they are unsure.)
- Were there sounds you heard that you had never heard before?
- Can you re-create any of the sounds made?

Sample of what an observation may look like

September 24, 9:00 a.m.

Cheese-bur-ger cheese-bur-ger – chickadee – song

Tweet tweet tweet – sparrow – song?

Jeer – blue jay – alarm

Caw Caw Caw – crow – alarm because we were in the woods

Extensions

- Consider having your students share their knowledge with another class by creating a presentation about bird language. Students love sharing their newfound abilities to understand the birds!
- Repeat this activity several times over the month or year. You will be surprised at how fast you and your students can understand bird language!

Bird behavior

Bird watching is a fantastic way to learn about the behavior of birds. Learning how and why animals behave helps us better understand human behavior as well (see Figure 4.24).

Figure 4.24 Observing birds
Source: Rachel Tidd

Materials

- A place to observe birds
- Bird field guide
- *Bird Behavior* worksheet, available at discoverwildlearning.com/
  wild-learning-book-resources
- Pencil
- Optional: binoculars

Activity

In this activity, children will observe bird behavior and record their observations. They will be looking for and recording information about bird
behaviors that they observe such as:

- Walking/branch hopping
- Feeding/drinking
- Preening/bathing
- Aggression or territorial behavior

- Nesting
- Mating/courtship
- Parenting
- Singing/alarm calls
- Flying
- Foraging
- Flocking

Give students a list of these bird behaviors and briefly discuss and solicit examples of each type of behavior from students. It can be fun to ask different groups of students to demonstrate each type of behavior by acting them out briefly in front of the class. To do this you can ask for volunteers or divide the class into groups and give each group a specific bird behavior for which to think of a way to "act it out" for the class. Then have groups take turns showing the class their "bird behaviors."

When finished presenting, hand out the behavior checklists and have students head out to observe bird behavior for 5–10 minutes (see Figure 4.25). They should be looking for as many different examples as they can during the allotted time. They should record the behavior, where they saw it, and the birds involved.

When the time is up, gather as a group and ask for students to share examples of each behavior. Discuss what surprised them or what they learned about bird behavior from this activity. What was the most common bird behavior they saw? The least common behavior?

Extension

Ask students to come up with a question about bird behavior that they can try to solve through more observations. After observing, students can then use their observations to try and answer the question. They can write a short lab report or paragraph describing their findings.

Track casting

This fun activity pairs well with "Tracks Tell a Story" in the "Reading and Writing Activities" section. Children love having their very own plaster cast of the animal tracks they found to take home!

Materials

- Plaster of Paris
- Access to animal tracks (creeks and other water bodies are great places to look)

Figure 4.25 Observing waterbirds
Source: Rachel Tidd

- Resealable sandwich bag for each track or child
- If the site has limited access to water, bring a jug or container filled with enough water to cast tracks for your students.
- Several ½-cup measuring cups
- Animal track field guide or resource
- Large container for transporting tracks safely

NOTE Plaster of Paris can be found at most home improvement or craft stores.

Preparation

Typically, plaster of Paris requires two parts plaster to one part water.

Place one cup of plaster in a resealable sandwich bag for each student.

You will need to take a total of one-half cup of water for each student. You can carry a gallon jug of water (ask students to help carry it) and measuring cup or bring only measuring cups with you if you plan on being near enough to a source of fresh water such as a creek, lake, or pond.

Activity

In this activity, children will use plaster of Paris to make a hard cast of an animal track. The best tracks for this activity are those that leave deep imprints in the mud or sand. An ideal place for track casting is in flat muddy areas near streams, ponds, or lakes. Animals are drawn to water, and the soft sand and mud found in these areas are the perfect medium for animal tracks (see Figure 4.26).

Have students work in groups looking for a good animal track for casting. Once a suitable track has been found, they can make a dam or barrier around the track using sand/mud to hold the plaster. When the dam is finished, they can pour one-half cup of water into the bag containing the plaster and mix. Once the plaster is mixed, they have about 5–10 minutes to pour and work with it. Make sure to emphasize that they should not mix their plaster until they are ready to pour it into the track!

After they pour the mixture of plaster and water into the track, they should use a stick to spread it evenly in the area around the track and up to the sides of the dam. It will take about 20–30 minutes to harden. When the plaster has almost hardened, have them use a thin stick to write their name or initials on the back carefully. Once the plaster has fully hardened, they can remove the sand dam and carefully lift out the plaster mold. They can scrape some of the sand and dirt off with their finger and carefully transport it back to the classroom. You may wish to have a plastic container or bucket to transport the tracks home safely.

If students are careful and the animal track holds up, more than one student can use it for casting. If there are not enough tracks for each student to make a cast, have students work in groups and display the casts in the classroom for everyone to enjoy.

While students wait for the plaster to harden and others to have their turn, have them use field guides to identify the tracks they found. They should also record the date and location of the tracks. They can also record facts from the field guide about the animal that made them. Once back in the classroom, place the tracks in a safe place to dry fully.

Figure 4.26 Raccoon tracks left in the mud
Source: Rachel Tidd

The YouTube video on track casting from MyNatureApps is helpful:
https://youtu.be/Y4WTmgo4zeA

Developing a Sit Spot Practice

Taking time to slow down and connect with the natural world can be challenging in our day-to-day lives. Sit spots are simply a spot to sit and quietly observe nature. They can be anywhere that a bit of nature can be observed. Some good locations are the base of a tree, a park bench, a porch or balcony, a backyard corner, up on a tree branch, a picnic table, or a rock by a stream. Each location will reveal its own unique secrets.

Students will develop a deeper connection to nature and hone their observation skills by noticing and tracking changes and paying attention to the small details, such as who lives and grows at their particular spot.

Students will return to this special spot throughout the year, noticing new changes and focusing on a different element. A sit spot can be meditative and help children relieve stress.

Sit spot journaling

By journaling about sit spots, students create a record of their observations. These journal entries can help them notice subtle changes and remember observations over the year. Children love looking back at their sit spot journal entries at the end of the year and marveling at all the changes that took place.

Materials

- Pencil
- Notebook
- Sit spot location

Activity

Explain what a sit spot is to your students and ask them to find their special place. Make sure to clearly define how far children may venture to find their spots (see Figure 4.27). Once everyone has found their spot, announce it is time to start. Have students sit in the spot and observe for at least five minutes. You may need to work up to a longer observation time. Start by observing for only a few minutes and over time gradually increase the time.

After five minutes, have students note any animals they have seen, plants growing there, the weather, sounds they may have heard, etc. These observations can be as detailed as they like. Modify your requirements based on the age and writing level of your students.

Afterward, have students share some of their observations with the whole class or in small groups. They can share what they saw and how they felt during this experience.

Questions that might help them reflect on their experience are:

- Did your feelings change as time progressed?
- Did you feel more relaxed?
- Did your mind wander?
- How did it feel to be alone in nature?

Variations

Writers for websites, social media, museum exhibits, and other public places often write descriptions of images for those that have visual

Figure 4.27 Students heading out to their sit spots
Source: Rachel Tidd

impairments. Have students describe their sit spot for someone who is visually impaired. Make sure they describe their location using multiple senses and as much detail as possible.

Mapping sit spots

When mapping a sit spot, students examine their sit spots through a new lens. They take their observations and translate them into map form. At the same time, they are applying concepts such as direction, scale, orientation, and more in the process.

Materials

- Pencil
- Notebook or paper
- Colored pencils
- Sit spot location

Activity

Begin by asking students to sit in their sit spot and observe for a few minutes. While observing, ask them to pay special attention to the main features of your spot. Is there a large oak tree on the left? A fence running behind it?

After observing for a few minutes, have them sketch a map of their sit spot location. Make sure they include all the major landmarks – trees, streams, fences, bushes, paths, where you are sitting, buildings, if any, etc.

Once students have drawn the major landmarks, encourage them to add details such as plants, flowers, and any animal friends that often visit their spot. Finally, have students add labels to all the main features of their sit spot and add color (see Figure 4.28).

Adjusting the activity

Encourage older students to consider using a rough scale to make their map more accurate and to add details such as a compass rose.

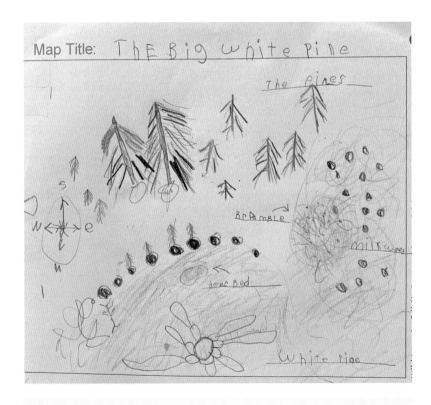

Figure 4.28 A student map of their sit spot
Source: Rachel Tidd

Sit spot news

Students always love this activity because they can pretend they are reporters for a newspaper. They use their observations to create headlines and/or write short articles for their imaginary newspaper.

Materials

- Pencil
- Paper or *Sit Spot Times* worksheet, available at discoverwildlearning .com/wild-learning-book-resources
- Sit spot location

Activity

Pose this question to your students: If there was a newspaper that covered the events and changes in your sit spot, what would the headlines be? When students observe their sit spots today, have them view their spot through the lens of a reporter (see Figure 4.29).

After making their observations, students will use them to write head-lines for a newspaper. Explain that headlines are like the title of a

Figure 4.29 Writing sit spot news headlines
Source: Rachel Tidd

book: They help draw a reader's attention to what is happening in the city, town, or in this case, their sit spot! After observing, you may have students simply record their headlines on paper or use the *Sit Spot Times* worksheet to record their headlines and draw a picture of one of the events (see Figure 4.30).

Questions that may help them when observing their sit spots

- What changes have there been?
- Are there any signs of a changing season?
- Are some plants no longer at their peak and others now blooming?
- What visitors have you seen today?
- What are the current weather conditions?

Figure 4.30 Student work example: Sit Spot Times
Source: Rachel Tidd

Example headlines

- Sparrow Rushes to Finish Nest!
- First Frost Kills Flowers!
- Maples Put on Fiery Display for Autumn!

Adjusting the activity

You can take this activity to the next level by having students choose one of their headlines and write a short article about it. Combine articles from the class to make a class newspaper!

Sit spot as the setting

When writing a story, we often begin with creating the plot or characters. In this activity, students will instead use their sit spot as a setting to inspire a story.

Materials

- Pencil
- Paper
- Sit spot location

Activity

After a few minutes of observations at their sit spots, ask students to create a story that takes place in their sit spot. It can be in any style or genre they wish! The only requirement is that the story's setting is their sit spot.

After writing, have some students share their pieces with the class. The creative ways that children weave the sit spots into stories are entertaining and can inspire their classmates' writing. This may be an activity you wish to repeat more than once (see Figure 4.31).

Adjusting the activity

- Beginning writers may draw a picture of the story at their sit spot, then work on the writing portion in a subsequent outdoor session or during writing time in the classroom.
- Provide graphic organizers to help students brainstorm and organize the major parts of the story.
- Have students revise and fine-tune their stories until they have a polished final version.

Figure 4.31 Sit spots are also a great activity in the winter
Source: Rachel Tidd

Final Thoughts

While taking your class on expeditions farther afield requires a little more planning and preparation, the learning opportunities and experiences they provide students are worth it. Activities such as sled races and writing in sit spots provide students the chance to immerse themselves in an activity and learn from it. These special lessons and trips will be what your students will remember long after their year with you! In the next chapter, you will learn how to bring a little nature inside your classroom through classroom routines and activities.

Inviting Nature Indoors

05

Time spent inside the classroom learning about nature and the outdoors is an excellent way for children to build upon their knowledge and experiences outdoors while fostering curiosity and wonder for the natural world. You can cultivate a classroom culture that is curious about and values nature by noticing seasonal rhythms, sharing nature observations, and integrating nature-inspired routines. Many of these activities can easily be incorporated into your existing morning meeting or closing circle routines. Other activities, such as creating a class nature journal, only require a weekly or monthly commitment. Choose activities that work best for your students, grade level, and geographical location.

A Nature-inspired Class Meeting

Drawing children's attention to the natural world during morning meetings is one of the simplest ways to integrate nature into your classroom. Your morning or class meeting likely already includes opportunities for students to participate in the meeting and a morning calendar routine. This section gives examples of incorporating observations of nature and seasonal cycles into your existing morning meeting and calendar routine. Consider holding your class meeting outdoors when possible! (See Figure 5.1.)

Sharing gratitude and nature sightings

Many classrooms have morning or afternoon routines that involve children each sharing something with the entire class. These activities are excellent ways to engage all students in the class and foster community. The daily practice of students sharing a single gratitude or nature sighting is an excellent way to build a community that cares about and respects the earth.

Activity: Sharing gratitude

During your class meeting time or when wrapping up the day, have children sit in a circle and take turns sharing a personal gratitude from the

Figure 5.1 Children participating in a flannel board activity during an outdoor morning meeting at PS 185 – The Locke School of Arts & Engineering in Harlem, New York
Source: Teresa Bello

day. It can be anything they wish. You will find that children come up with all kinds of examples of gratitude. If they are at a loss, suggest choosing something from nature such as the sun, the birds singing in the morning, or the fresh apple they had for lunch.

Activity: Sharing nature sightings

Sharing nature sightings is another way to involve each child in morning meetings while encouraging a deeper connection with the natural world. For this activity, ask children to share a nature sighting they may have seen that day or during the week. These sightings do not have to be elaborate. They can be as simple as hearing a sparrow in the bushes, the sun coming through the window while they ate breakfast, or listening to the rustle of leaves as the wind blew them across the sidewalk.

Alternatively, you may devote a few minutes during the day to ask if anyone has any nature sightings that they wish to share. This can also be a great way to fill in an awkward time in the schedule or to slowly release students to line up or begin the next activity.

Variation

Have children journal about something they are grateful for. This can be a perfect assignment for older children to work on as morning work or as a reflective way to end the day.

Outdoor Learning Tip: Nature Objects In-class Meetings and Discussions

Passing a special natural object such as a shell or a decorated stick around the circle during sharing activities can help keep children on task. The object or stick serves as a physical reminder that the only person who should be talking is the person holding the object.

The teachers at the former Lantern School at Earth Arts in Ithaca, New York, had a special basket full of natural objects such as rocks, shells, acorns, and feathers that children passed around. After they shared their gratitude, the student chose an object and placed it in the center of the circle (see Figure 5.2).

At the end of your meeting, choose one or two students to collect the special nature items and return them to the box, shelf, or basket where they are stored.

Figure 5.2 Nature items placed by students around a wooden box after sharing their gratitude during morning meeting
Source: Rachel Tidd

Weekly birdcall

Children love learning new birdcalls! By featuring a new birdcall each week, your students will gain extensive knowledge of different birds and their calls! It is so fun to witness their excitement when they recognize a birdcall outdoors or share an experience during circle time!

Materials

- Bird field guide
- A book such as *Backyard Birdsongs* by Donald Kroodsma or an app such as the free Merlin app by The Lab of Ornithology at Cornell University at https://merlin.allaboutbirds.org/

Activity

Each week, select a bird species that is local to your geographic area. Research a few interesting facts about the bird and locate a picture. This information is easily found in a field guide or online. Locate a recording of the birdcall.

During the meeting, play the sound for the class. Remind them that if they think they know what bird it is, they should not shout it out, so that others can listen. Play the song several times. Then you may ask the group if anyone guesses what bird makes the sound they just heard! After hearing a few responses, reveal the bird's identity, show the picture, and share a few facts with the class.

For the remainder of the week, play the birdcalls during meetings. You can also share more facts about the feature bird or review past birdsongs as time allows.

Extensions

- Occasionally review and do a quick informal birdsong quiz to see how many songs they can remember/identify!
- Find books and resources about the bird of the week and place them in the classroom library for children to explore.
- Students can further research the bird during the week in writer's workshop or science.

Calendar of firsts

Watching the seasons change can be a magical experience for children. We often notice the events marking seasonal shifts such as the first snow or summer vacation, but do your students notice the smaller hints that time is passing? Do they note the first time a robin appears in spring or the first tinge of orange in the maple tree in the fall? By keeping track of these "firsts," students will expand their awareness of the relationship between the cycle of the seasons, time, and the calendar year. If your geographical location does not have four distinct seasons, subtle changes can still be found that showcase the passage of time and the cyclical way they happen each year. This type of activity gains momentum with time and ignites excitement in a classroom with children eagerly observing nature at home and school hoping to spot a first and share with the class!

Materials

- Chart paper or large blank calendar for recording observations

Activity

Introduce the idea of a calendar of firsts to your class by modeling something that you noticed during the past week or two that is an excellent example of a "first." A first is when you observe something for the first time that is a sign of the forthcoming season. For example, in the spring, you might glimpse the green tips of the daffodils poking through the leaves after the snow melts. This is an excellent example of a first because it is a sign that spring is on the way and is the first time you have observed it this year. Other examples might be a dandelion blossom, frost, pumpkins for sale, icicles dripping, or buds plumping on branches of trees in the spring.

Decide how you would like to record these firsts throughout the year. The simplest way is by making a list on chart paper and listing the date. You can record the firsts from each month and then display the past months or bind them into a large book. Some teachers like to record them on a large blank calendar. Dedicating a bulletin board to this project and constructing a timeline can also be a unique way to display the data.

Students can occasionally become overcompetitive in finding the firsts. This can be mitigated by recording the student's name next to the observation and making sure to call on different students each time you add to the list. By recording the name next to the student's observation, you can easily track who has yet to share. Placing a checklist of student names on the back of the chart can be helpful.

At the beginning of each month or the official start of a new season, spend a few minutes looking back at the list of observations and invite students to reflect on their observations. Ask questions such as, What do they notice? Were there lots of signs that the season was changing or only a few? Was there a time when there were many firsts and other periods with only a few?

Figure 5.3 A student's calendar of firsts
Source: Rachel Tidd

The answers to these questions will vary with your geographical location. Sometimes what we observe does not match up to the date on a calendar or a current year's weather pattern. Where I live in the Northeastern United States, signs of spring can be hard to find on the spring equinox! Yet, if I look beyond the snow on the ground, I often see small signs that spring is on its way.

Variations

- **Individual calendars:** Having students keep their calendar of firsts can be a wonderful extension of this activity. Print blank calendars and have children fill in their observations of firsts (see Figure 5.3).
- **Narrative writing:** The first signs of the seasons can make an excellent topic for narrative writing. Ask students to expand on this small moment using descriptive language.

Tracking the weather

Observing and tracking the weather is a great way for children to begin noticing the natural world around them. Weather can affect what we wear, our activities outdoors, if school is closed or open, and even how we feel!

Keeping track of the weather changes is an excellent opportunity to integrate math and science concepts into your morning routine. Consider tracking temperature, measuring precipitation, or tallying the number of sunny vs. cloudy days. Upper grade students can track percent humidity, wind speed, and atmospheric pressure.

Materials

- Outdoor thermometer(s)
- Rain gauge (DIY or store-bought)
- Large graph on chart paper or interactive whiteboard
- Clipboard
- Simple data recording sheets (date and measurement for each)
- Advanced weather data such as humidity, wind speed, and atmospheric pressure can readily be found on the internet or from a weather station in the schoolyard

Activity: Graphing weather statistics

Recording data and constructing a class graph can be a fantastic way for your students to practice graphing skills in a practical, real-life context.

This activity works best if the data is collected by a student in the morning before the morning meeting. Appointing a daily or weekly "Weather Reporter" allows each student in the class to collect and graph data multiple times over the school year. Before the meeting, the students collect weather data and record them on a data sheet. Using a simple data sheet will guide students when recording and graphing the data and provide a historical record of all the data. This record is a helpful reference when presenting to the class, as well as a physical record of measurements over time. During the morning meeting, the weather reporter shares the day's weather statistics and adds them to the graph and/or calendar.

Adjusting this activity

For lower grades, have students measure and record the temperature, note the amount of precipitation, and observe if the day is sunny or cloudy. Creating a line graph on chart paper or an interactive whiteboard that students add to each day works well. Using a line graph to track temperature, a bar graph to track precipitation, and a tally chart to track sunny vs. cloudy days give students practice with reading and graphing three different graph types.

In the upper grades, the weather report can be more complex. Measuring the percent humidity, wind speed, and atmospheric pressure connects science and higher-level math concepts such as percent, speed, weather fronts, and pressure. You may wish to integrate different statistics as they are introduced in math or science. For example, you may have students begin tracking percent humidity after introducing percentages in math class to provide real-life practice using and interpreting percentages. Be sure to periodically examine and discuss the data, asking students to look for patterns or changes. Encourage them to make weather predictions or forecasts and use the data to support any predictions. For example, after looking closer at the data, students may notice that the weather becomes drier and sunnier after the pressure rises and steadies.

Variation

Weather observations are an excellent activity for all children to complete in the morning before the morning meeting. For this, create packets with monthly data sheets and graph outlines for students in lower grades or who need more support and graph paper, Excel, or Google Sheets for recording weather statistics. Some teachers find it helpful to put weather data on the interactive whiteboard for students to record in their booklets. In this scenario the weather reporter simply reviews the data during the morning meeting and may add in their interpretations such as, "The pressure is dropping, and there is a lot of wind. I think there might be a storm coming!"

Cultivating Nature Appreciation and Curiosity Throughout the Year

Working on an ongoing nature-based project can be a great way to invite nature into the classroom all year long while not requiring a daily time commitment. Yearlong projects help build continuity through the year and help children notice, experience, and make connections between the year's natural cycles.

Outdoor Learning Tip: Classroom Nature Library

Having books, field guides, and other resources about your local habitat, animals, and plants will encourage students to seek answers to their questions about nature through reading and research. Display books in your classroom library that reflect the current season and topics your students may encounter during your outdoor lessons. (See Figure 5.4.)

Figure 5.4 A classroom display of nature books
Source: Rachel Tidd

Creating a class nature journal

Creating a class book that records nature sightings and observations, reports on treasures found and samples collected on nature walks or field trips, documents a significant or exciting weather event, and other shared nature experiences help make nature study a part of the community and classroom culture.

This activity pairs well with individual nature journals. It allows students to contribute to a larger classwide project in the form of the classroom book as well as record personal experiences in their nature journals.

Materials

- A class book (this can be a sizeable blank notebook or artist sketchbook, or thick paper bound together with binder rings or placed in a binder; 9 × 12 inches or larger works well)
- Old magazines with nature or animal photos for cutting and pasting
- Access to a printer or provide printed photos to add to the book
- Heavy books, or flower press for pressing flowers and other natural specimens to add to the book
- Glue sticks or tape
- Colored pencils or markers

Activity

Class nature journals can take many forms and sizes. A larger format provides plenty of room for children to write, draw, and add pressed plant samples, photos, or magazine clippings. This larger-sized book also allows multiple children to work on or read the book simultaneously. Pages may be left blank with the design of each page left up to the students or you may wish to provide more structure by having lines for writing and an area designated for art, samples, and photos.

Once you have obtained or constructed the blank book, model how to create a page based on a nature experience that the class shared. You can make the example page ahead of time and simply share your entry, your process, and its components with the class or model creating the page and taking suggestions from the class on what to include and explaining components and options as you go (see Figure 5.5).

Once students have an idea of what the potential is for the book, there are several different ways that you can integrate the project into class time:

- After a nature walk, choose a few students to work on the class book, while the rest of the class works on recording their experiences in their nature journals.
- Provide time for rotating groups of students to work on the book during writing workshop, morning work, or science. It often is best to have only two to three students working together on the book at a time.

Figure 5.5 An example page from a class nature journal
Source: Rachel Tidd

- Allow students to add to the book if they finish work early or during "free time."
- Allow students to read the book during silent reading time, free time, morning time, etc.
- Display the book in the classroom for children and visitors to see!
- Notice and share ideas to put in the book when outside, on nature walks or when sharing nature sightings. For example, you might say to your class, "How exciting that we saw a flock of geese flying south today during our neighborhood walk! What a fantastic sign that fall is coming! We should record this in our Class Nature Book!" Then follow up by providing time for a few students to record the sighting.

After pointing out and recording several examples, you will notice that your students will start making suggestions about what to put in the book and take more ownership of the project. Encourage their enthusiasm by providing time and space for recording and creating these nature experiences. If many students have ideas all at once, encourage them to make a rough draft of what they want to include (to serve as a model when it is their turn to work on the book) or make their entry in their nature journal. Once you fill one book up, create another and introduce the idea of volumes to your students.

Extension

Have groups share the pages they created with the class to practice public speaking skills!

Creating self-portraits with natural materials

Many teachers begin the school year by having children construct self-portraits. Elementary students are typically starting to develop their self-concept and understand their personal strengths. This project is a beautiful way to gain insight by seeing the child through their eyes. Here we give self-portraits a nature-inspired twist by using natural materials (see Figure 5.6).

Materials:

- Natural materials (such as sticks, grass, flowers, moss, pinecones, small rocks, and seeds)
- Containers to gather materials in (recycled containers such as gallon milk jugs with the top cut off or sour cream containers with the top work well)
- Glue
- Cardstock or pieces of upcycled cardboard
- Optional: small mirrors or several mirrors for children to see their reflection

Activity

Prepare for this activity by gathering cardstock or upcycled cardboard pieces and containers for children to collect materials. You can also ask children to look for and collect natural materials at home and bring them in. Before beginning, ensure that you have a safe space to spread out the self-portraits for them to dry.

Explain to your students that they will collect natural materials from the schoolyard and neighborhood to construct a self-portrait. Share an example or model making your self-portrait using natural materials. Allow children ample time to create their self-portraits.

Figure 5.6 Self-portrait created using natural materials
Source: Rachel Tidd

After they have completed their self-portrait, have students add writing to the piece. If needed, provide a sentence starter such as, "Three words that describe me are . . ." Older students may write a paragraph or two describing their personalities, likes, dislikes, and hobbies.

Extensions

- **Year-end reflection:** Consider repeating this activity at the end of the year. Save or take digital pictures of each self-portrait, including any writing. At the end of the year, have children create another self-portrait and writing piece. When finished, show them their work from the beginning of the year. Have them reflect on what aspects have changed and what has remained the same. How has their appearance changed? What about their description? Has their art technique or writing improved? This is an excellent activity for students to see tangible evidence of personal growth!

- **Earth-based professional artist:** Artist Andy Goldsworthy uses natural materials to make art. You may wish to introduce some of his art to your students. Find more about Andy Goldsworthy from this article on the *Living Your Wild Creativity* website at https://www.livingyourwild-creativity.com/art-gallery-1-mitchell-
- **Read aloud:** *The Anywhere Artist* by Nikki Slade Robinson

Create a classroom nature collection

Devoting a space in your classroom to a nature collection is a physical way to show students that you value nature and think it's important. Encouraging students to add to the collection as the year progresses creates excitement about nature that is contagious (see Figure 5.7)!

Materials

- A space to devote to the nature museum or collection such as a few shelves, table, bulletin board, or windowsills
- Index cards or slips of paper for labeling specimens
- Container, or a small basket to hold blank notecards

Figure 5.7 Example of a nature collection
Source: Rachel Tidd

Outdoor Learning Tip: Respecting Nature When Collecting

Collecting common nature items is a fantastic learning opportunity for your students. Collecting nature items can be controversial. One point of view is that we should leave no trace when venturing into nature. Another view is if everyone took something home with them, then there would not be anything left. While these are valid and important concerns, in this context, we are collecting items to learn more about them, just as scientists do. Discuss respectful ways to collect nature treasures with your class. Consider returning the items to their locations at the end of the year or when you are finished studying them.

- Do not collect live animals.
- Collect only abundant items and consider returning items to the location when finished studying them or at the end of the school year.
- Make sure you are collecting things you are legally allowed to collect and where it is legal to collect. (In some locations, the collection of feathers and fossils is restricted; for example, collecting items in national parks is not allowed.)
- Do not taste or put items in your mouth.
- Respect private property.
- Collect leaves, nuts, flowers, and pinecones that have fallen on the ground.

- Completed notecards for your students to serve as a model for completing their own
- Small containers, bowls, baskets, and jars to hold specimens
- Field guides are helpful to have available for children to identify their specimens and find the scientific name
- Optional materials: magnifying glass, ruler, microscope

Activity

Begin by identifying and creating a space for the nature collection. Shallow shelves and windowsills work particularly well. Make sure to account for the future growth of the collection!

Decide if you want this to be a "museum" where children look at the items mostly with their eyes or a "collection" that they are allowed to touch and interact with. Choose what works best for your classroom. Whichever approach you take, discuss any expectations with the class. If touching materials is permitted, it is wise to lead a class discussion about being gentle with the materials, noting the possibility that some objects could accidentally get broken.

Once you have identified an area to display the collection, find and add some nature treasures of your own. They can be simple objects such as acorns, pinecones, feathers, and pretty rocks. You may wish to also add in some more unique finds such as bird nests, rocks, crystals, bones, etc. Part of the fun is finding new things to add to the collection! You just need a few things to start the collection so that children can get excited about the project!

Fill out an index card for some of your nature finds. These can include the date, the item's name, scientific name if applicable, where it was found, and who found it (see Figure 5.8). These cards will serve as models for students to complete their own cards.

Place a small container with index cards nearby. These index cards will serve as a way for children to add labels to items they wish to add to

Figure 5.8 Have students use index cards to label nature items in the classroom
Source: Rachel Tidd

Books to Inspire Your Collectors!

- *Cabinet of Curiosities: Collecting and Understanding the Wonders of the Natural World* by Gordon Grice
- *Too Many Stones* by David L. Krieger
- *What's in Your Pocket? Collecting Nature's Treasures* by Heather Montgomery
- *The Pinecone Walk* by Barbara Springfield
- *Trees, Leaves, Flowers and Seeds: A Visual Encyclopedia of the Plant Kingdom* by DK
- *Roxaboxen* by Alice McLerran
- *Collections* by Margaret Ballinger and Rachel Gosset
- *Hannah's Collections* by Marthe Jocelyn
- *The Button Box* by Margarette Reid
- *If You Find a Rock* by Peggy Christian

the collection. Placing a model card nearby or hanging it above the container helps students to complete cards independently.

When you are ready to introduce the idea of a classroom nature collection to your students, consider introducing the concept of nature collecting by reading one or both of the following books aloud to the class.

- *The Collectors* by Alice Feagan
- *What's in Your Pocket? Collecting Nature's Treasures* by Heather Montgomery

Next, give your students a tour of the classroom collection or museum area, and explain that this is the class's nature museum. Invite children to bring in nature finds that they find at home, on nature walks, or during outdoor time at school. Explain how to fill out a card for a specimen and why they are helpful. Discuss whether the materials in the class collection are for looking at like in a museum or if they will be able to touch them. You may also wish to lead a discussion about some simple guidelines and ways to respect nature when collecting (see the Outdoor Learning Tip: Respecting Nature When Collecting).

If you find your collection beginning to take over your classroom, consider cleaning it out every few months or seasonally. Send the specimens and their cards home with students or return them to the natural environment.

Using natural materials for classroom activities

Bringing natural materials inside the classroom is a great way to encourage children to use, learn more about, and observe these materials in different ways. Natural materials can be used as manipulatives in math lessons or centers instead of plastic materials. You can include natural materials in literacy and writing centers, independent work choices, and science areas. Adding natural materials to sensory bins and sand and water tables can be another fun way to incorporate natural materials if you have these areas in your classroom.

Materials

- Natural materials
- Trays and/or bins
- Paper with a question that invites the students to engage with the material

Activity

Set out some natural materials that you wish for your students to explore further or in a different way. For example, you may set out flowers for children on a table with a sign inviting them to make patterns or a variety of leaves and items found during a walk or prior activity outside (see Figures 5.9 and 5.10). This could be an option to work on during morning arrival, math centers, independent work time, or after finishing an activity.

Figure 5.9 An invitation for students to use flowers to make patterns
Source: Teresa Bello

Figure 5.10 Materials from an outdoor activity are set out on trays for further observation
Source: Teresa Bello

Variations

- **Montessori-style activity bins:** Create bins containing activities that incorporate natural materials. These bins can work well as an activity for children to work on as they arrive in the morning instead of traditional "bell work." Each student or pair of students selects a bin to work on. These boxes can also be used for early finishers, centers, or during choice time. (See Figure 5.11.)
- **Math manipulatives:** Using natural materials for math is not just for outside – you can bring them indoors as well! Try using them for lessons or centers instead of plastic manipulatives.
- **Sensory activities:** Many early childhood classrooms have sensory bins or sand and water tables. Try adding natural materials to these areas! Some fun ideas are acorns, pinecones, wood, and shells to the water table (some sink and some float!). Try seeds and dirt, petals and water, leaves, or rocks in sensory bins.
- **Science materials:** When possible, have materials that pertain to your science unit, nature study, or season available for exploration in your science area or other location in your classroom. Don't forget that you can also integrate them into science lessons! (See Figure 5.12.)

Phenology wheel

A phenology wheel is a simple way to document nature observations and seasonal changes. It shows the year in the form of a circle, highlighting

Figure 5.11 Montessori-style independent activity bins incorporating natural materials available for prekindergarten students at P.S. 185 – The Locke School of Arts & Engineering in Harlem, New York
Source: Teresa Bello

Figure 5.12 Natural materials available for student use in the science area of the classroom
Source: Teresa Bello

how the year's seasons are cyclical. Phenology wheels are easy to implement in your classroom because they only need to be completed once a month. This is an excellent way for children to reflect on nature sightings they had during the month or heard about during sharing time during a morning meeting. You may wish to devote a permanent place in your classroom to display the wheels and update them each month.

Materials

- Printed phenology wheel available at discoverwildlearning.com/wild-learning-book-resources
- Pencil
- Colored pencils or watercolors

Activity

Introduce the activity by explaining what a phenology wheel is. You can show students a finished example or some pictures of phenology wheels. Model filling in the current month and then have students complete their own. Keep the phenology wheels in a safe place or display them and revisit them each month. If starting at the beginning of the school year, you may wish to have students complete the prior months (summer vacation) so that the whole wheel will be completed at the end of the school year.

Adjusting this activity

Have older students construct their own phenology wheels using a compass and a ruler. This is a great way to integrate geometry and fractions. Adjust the guidance given for this activity based on the age and experience of the students. You may provide step-by-step directions with modeling or simply a few hints on how to do it and let the students figure it out!

Students can write a summary of their nature observations and seasonal changes for each month. At the end of the year, ask students to make a small book with their entries and phenology wheel (see Figure 5.13).

Final Thoughts

This chapter shows how integrating nature-inspired routines such as daily gratitude and creating a class nature collection into your classroom is a powerful way to support your work outside the classroom. It creates a classroom culture that values curiosity and encourages investigating our questions about what we observe, read, and wonder in order to build knowledge and understanding. Tracking the weather and seasonal changes helps children appreciate the natural world and notice the subtle changes as time passes. Providing resources in a nature library, such

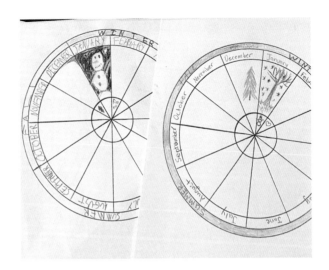

Figure 5.13 Examples of phenology wheels
Source: Rachel Tidd

as books and field guides, can help children make connections between texts, outdoor lessons, and life experiences.

I hope this book has shown you how to teach core subjects such as math, reading, and writing in the schoolyard, the neighborhood, and farther afield and the many benefits that your students gain when you do so. Outdoor learning is not limited to special outdoor classroom spaces, science topics, special programs, trips, or specialized curricula. You can take advantage of the outdoor environments available near your school by making slight modifications to your current lessons and curriculum. When you take your class outdoors, your students are more engaged and attentive, and their mood often improves. The outdoor environment and activities help you provide movement and multisensory learning opportunities in ways that are difficult to replicate inside the classroom. Effective lessons are not limited to the indoor classroom – taking your lessons outside can have immediate and long-lasting effects for your students' health and learning. I urge you to tell your class to put on their coats, grab a notebook and pencil, and take your learning outside!

Acknowledgments

First and foremost, I would like to thank my boys, Finn and Taro, who inspired me to take teaching outdoors in the first place! Thank you for your endless patience, willingness to test activities, and for letting me take so many photos!

Special thanks to Teresa Bello from P.S. 185 – The Locke School of Arts & Engineering in Harlem, New York; Andrew Chiappetta and Greta Schwerner from P.S. 146 – The Brooklyn New School in Brooklyn, New York; and Angie Wright from Lincoln City Christian School in Lincoln City, Oregon for contributing photos. Much gratitude to Julie Manners, for helping me with the zone graphic. My deep gratitude to the many parents who allowed me to use photographs of their children in this book. I would like to thank Natalie Muñoz, Associate Editor at Jossey-Bass, for initially reaching out to me about writing this book, and the whole Wiley/Jossey-Bass team for their enthusiasm and hard work in getting this book out and into teachers' hands.

Thank you to Elizabeth Bazett Perry, for telling me years ago that I needed to write these ideas down and share them. To all the teachers and parents who have used my Wild Math and Wild Reading curriculums, thank you for your feedback, encouragement, and support. Without it, the vision for this book would never have happened.

Finally, I would like to thank my husband, Leo, for his endless patience, support, editing, and feedback during the process of writing this book. Thanks for always believing in me and encouraging me to write this book from the very beginning.

About the Website

The below worksheets are available on **discoverwildlearning.com/wild-learning-book-resources**

Phenology Wheels
Bird Behavior
Sit Spot Times
How Seeds Spread Scavenger Hunt

Index

A

Accessibility, zones of 4–11
Addition activities 37, 38, 58, 74, 76, 77, 79, 158
Affixes 45–46
Afield, exploring 150–196
  learning tips for 156, 167
  sit spot practice for 189–196
  and studies beyond natural areas 151
  using plants/animals for 150–189
Alphabets:
  collecting 167–169
  movable 70–74
Angles 58, 81, 109, 110
Animals 150–189
  and living in trees 129
  and math activities 150–167
  and reading/writing activities 167–177
  and science activities 177–189
Answers, rocks to record 74
Arborist activity 130
Area 43–44, 88
Arrays 81–82, 113–114
Art 48–49, 161
Atmospheric pressure, tracking 203–204
Attitude, increasing positive 3, 30

B

Base layers 24, 27–28
Bean bag toss game 54–56

Behavior, and outdoor learning 3
Bio blitzes 182
Birds 94–96, 182–186, 199–200
Block play activity 119
Bloom, calendar of 159–161
Books. *See also* Read-alouds
  on birds 96
  classroom tree 132
  and cloud observations 103
  on graffiti 49
  to inspire nature collectors 213
  on nature journaling 135
  on personification 146
  on positive outdoor experiences 30
  pressed flower fact 157
  and procedural writing 104
  and reading outdoors 23
  on seeds 180
  simile and metaphor 170
  on snowflakes 100
  on snow people 164
  on sticks 156
  on street art/graffiti 49
  on trees 129
  in unexpected places 120
Brooklyn New School 151

C

Calendars, making 159–161, 200–202
Casting 186–189
Cemeteries 144–145

Chalk 34–51
    cleanup considerations for 36
    math activities using 34–44
    reading/writing activities
        using 44–51
Change a letter game 62–65, 72
Characters 93
Checklists, visual 26
Circumference 111
Citizen science projects 95
Class meetings 197–204
Classroom management 19–21
Clay characters 93
Cloud stories 102–104
Cold conditions 28, 167
Collect 100 activity 36, 152–155
Collections, making 68–69,
        152–155, 210–213
Combinations, learning 36
Communication, with guardians 19
Community involvement 131, 145,
        197–199
Complex words 46
Contractions 90–92
Conversions 117
Counting, skip 36, 38, 52–54,
        76–78, 114–116, 156–159
Crazy boards activity 61
Creative thinking 168, 172–177
Crossword games 72
Culture, building classroom 9, 197

D
Data collection 94, 161
Decimals 38, 113
Density 100–102
Descriptive writing 136, 147,
        148–149
Details 136

Dichotomous keys 177–179
Direction 191–192
Discussions, nature objects
        for 199
Distances, measuring 116–117
Documentation, of outside
        work 38
Doors, activities using 139
Dots and shapes activity 57
Drawing 135
Drinks, warm 167

E
Earth Arts 199
Earth-based professional
        artists 210
Elimination (math fact toss-up
        variation) 56
Elkonin boxes 72
Engagement, outdoor learning
        for 1, 2, 10
Equivalent fractions,
        modeling 84–87
Estimation 145
Even numbers activity 78, 112
Expanded form 155–157
Experiences, positive
        outdoor 29–30
Experts, in classrooms 125–131
Expository writing skills 177

F
Fact families 74
Facts, modeling math 35
Fear, reducing 29, 30
Firsts, calendar of 200–202
Flowers, using 74–76, 150, 152,
        156–161
Force, activities to learn 98

Fractions 38, 58, 82–87, 217
Free writes 137–138
Friction 98

G
Games:
   for math 51–59
   memory 70
   for reading/writing 59–68
Gear 21, 24–29
General activities:
   leaf flower sorts 74–76
   letter and number rocks
     70–74
   using natural materials
     for 69–76
Geometry, learning 80–81,
     99–100, 106–111, 150,
     152, 217
Graffiti, word 48–50
Graphemes 46–48, 62–65
Graphing 94, 164
Gratitude, class meetings for
     197–199
Graveyards 144–145
Grouping 113–114, 158

H
Hands-on learning 1, 4
Handwriting 72
Headlines, creating 193–195
High-frequency words 48–50,
     59–62, 67, 73
History 51, 66
Homophones 67–68
Hopscotch games 60–62
Hot weather, gear for 28
Humidity 203–204
Hundred chart 152–155

I
Imagination, using 139
Indoors, inviting nature
     197–218
   class meetings for 197–204
   learning tips for 199, 205, 211
   yearlong projects for
     204–217
   as zone of accessibility 9–10
Inferences 172–174
Insects 129, 180–182
Inside-Out organization 30

J
Journaling:
   about gratitude 198
   nature 135, 158, 161,
     205–208
   in sit spots 190–191
Jump rope activity 54

L
Language, learning bird 183
Lantern School (Earth Arts) 199
Lattice multiplication 41–42
Leaf flower sorts 74–76
Leafixes activity 92
Leaf sorts 70
Learning styles 1, 2
Learning tips:
   for exploring afield 156, 167
   for inviting nature indoors 199,
     205, 211
   for neighborhoods 107, 109,
     120, 131, 135, 144
   for planning/preparation 23,
     25–26, 32
   for schoolyards 36, 38, 40, 78,
     82, 94, 100

Leaves:
   resources 125
   using 74–76, 90–92, 123–125,
      156–159, 174–175
Lessons, class schedule for
     various 22
Letters, learning 44–46, 62–65,
     70–74, 118–119
Libraries:
   nature 205
   outdoor gear 25
Lines, number 37–40
Loads, experimenting with
     different 98
Locations, choosing 8–9, 13–17,
     67, 131

M
Machines, activity about
     simple 98
Management, classroom 19–21
Manhattan New School 151
Mapmaking 121–123
Maps, of sit spots 191–192
Marking up words 72–73
Masks activity 88–89
Matching 70
Materials:
   natural (see Natural materials)
   for outdoors 15–16
   planning/preparation of 30–33
Math activities:
   area method of multiplication
     43–44
   bean bag toss 54–56
   calculating water in snow
     100–102
   calendar of bloom 159–161
   in cemeteries/graveyards 144

   collect 100 natural items
     152–155
   creating arrays 81–82
   designing playgrounds 96–97
   finding arrays/groups during
     113–114
   flower geometry 150, 152
   hopscotch 62
   investigating
     snowflakes 99–100
   lattice multiplication 41–42
   to learn geometry 106–111
   math fact toss-up 56–57
   to measure distances 116–117
   measuring snow people
     164–167
   modeling fractions 82–87
   in natural areas 109
   natural materials for 215
   number ladders 39–41
   number lines 37–39
   number-themed 111–113
   physics on the
     playground 97–99
   place value sticks 76–80
   in schoolyards 93–94, 96–102
   scoot game 57–58
   skip counting 52–54, 114–116
   sledding races 161–164
   snowball target 58–59
   stick geometry 80–81
   ten frames 35–37
   3D shapes in snow 87–88
   using chalk 34–44
   using flowers/leaves 156–159
Math fact toss-up game 56–57
Measuring wheels 117
Meditation 129, 190
Meetings, class 197–204

Memory games 70
Mental health 1–2, 6
Mental math 39, 51
Metaphors 170
Mid-layers, insulating 24, 27, 28
Montessori-style activity bins 215
Movable letters 70–71
Mudpies 83–87
Multiplication 41–44, 52–54, 78,
    81–82, 156–159
Multisensory 1, 4, 34, 90, 218. *See
    also* Sensory
Museums, classroom nature
    211, 213

N
Narrative writing 202
Natural areas. *See also* Afield,
    exploring
  math walks in 109
  studies beyond 151
  as zone of accessibility 4, 8–9
Natural materials:
  additional ways to use 78
  in class meetings/
    discussions 199
  collecting 152–155
  to create storyboards 50–51
  general activities using 69–76
  math activities using 35, 76–88
  reading/writing activities
    using 88–93
  in schoolyards 68–93
  self-portraits with 208–210
  for yearlong projects 214–215
Nature:
  books to inspire collectors
    of 213
  connections, to nature 1, 9, 189

journaling 135, 158, 161,
    205–208
  respecting 211
  riddles about 139–141
  in unexpected places 119–121
Neighborhoods 105–149
  finding words in 118–119
  learning tips for 107, 109, 120,
    131, 135, 144
  odes to 147, 148–149
  walking adventures in 105–135
  as zone of accessibility 4, 6,
    8, 13
Notebooks, outdoor 32
Number bonds activity 78
Number ladders 39–41
Number lines 37–40
Number rocks 70–74
Numbers, learning 109, 113
Number sentences 73
Number-themed math walks
    111–113

O
Objects, nature 199
Observation skills 123–129,
    185–186, 189–191, 193–195
Odd numbers activities 78, 112
Order of operations 73
Orientation, learning about
    191–192
Outdoor learning tips
  alternative number line
    methods 40
  chalk cleanup considerations 36
  classroom nature library 205
  documenting outdoor work 38
  leaf sorts, matching, and
    memory games 70

Outdoor learning tips (*Continued*)
  making quality outdoor gear
    accessible for all 25
  math walks in natural
    environments 109
  more ways to use natural
    materials 78
  move independent reading
    outdoors 23
  nature journaling 135
  nature objects in class meetings
    and discussions 199
  outdoor notebooks 32
  portable writing surfaces 107
  recording work in wet or snowy
    conditions 94
  respecting nature when
    collecting 211
  stick safety 156
  using snow to make arrays 82
  utilizing cemeteries and
    graveyards 144
  utilizing community voices and
    resources 131
  warm drinks 167
  winter in the schoolyard 100
Outdoor notebooks 32
Outdoors, benefits of teaching 1–4
Outer layers, weatherproof
  24, 27, 28

P
Packets, seed 171–172
Paper, leaves as 76
Parental support, for outdoor
  learning 19
Parks 4, 8–9. *See also* Afield,
  exploring
Parts of speech activity 67

Patterns 214–215
Pendulums 98
Perimeter activity 80–81
Personification 146
Phenology wheels 215–217
Phonemes 46–48, 62–65,
  118–119, 168
Phonics 44–46, 48–50, 60–65,
  118–119, 145
Photo display activity 51
Physical health, from outdoor
  learning 1
Physics, on the playground 97–99
Picture card spelling 72
Place value 111, 113, 155–157
Place value sticks 76–80
Planning and preparation 13–33
  of gear 21, 23–29
  learning tips for 23, 25–26, 32
  of materials 30–33
  of outdoor locations 13–17
  and parental support 19
  for positive outdoor
    experiences 29–30
  safety considerations for 17–18
  sample outdoor class schedule
    for 22
  of time/classroom
    management 19–21
Plants 150–189
  classification of 72, 73, 177–179
  math activities using 150–167
  reading/writing activities using
    167–177
  science activities using 177–189
Plaster of Paris 187–188
Playacting 88–89
Playgrounds, using 65–67, 96–99
Portable writing surfaces 107

Predictions activity 161
Prefixes 45–46, 92
Procedural writing 103–104
Programs, outdoor 4
Public speaking skills 208
Punctuation 67–68
Puzzles, and word ladders 46–48

R
Races, sledding 161–164
Rainy conditions, gear for 28
Rate, investigating 99
Ratios 100–102
Read-alouds 120, 137, 148–149,
    210
Reading and writing activities. *See
    also* Writing activities
  building settings 175–177
  change a letter 62–65
  clay characters 93
  collect the alphabet 167–169
  creating a wild seed catalog
    170–172
  hopscotch 60–62
  leaf contractions 90–92
  leafixes 92
  from a leaf's perspective 174–175
  leaf syllables 90
  letter rocks 70–74
  to map neighborhoods 121–123
  masks and playacting 88–89
  and nature in unexpected places
    119–121
  playground words 65–67
  sentence challenge 67–68
  similes and metaphors 170
  storyboards 50–51
  storytelling with tracks 172–174
  using chalk 44–51

  word graffiti 48–50
  word ladders 46–48
  words in neighborhood 118–119
  word squares 44–46
  word tic-tac-toe 59–60
Reading comprehension 66, 89,
    106. *See also* Reading and
    writing activities
Reading outdoors 23
Reading words 65–67
Reflections, year-end 209
Research skills 123–125, 129, 144,
    145, 161
Resources:
  on bird languages 183
  on citizen science projects 95
  on dichotomous keys 178
  inventorying
    neighborhood's 105
  on leaf shapes 125
  on nature 135
  on read-alouds 137
  on seed catalogs 171
  utilizing community 131
  on word ladders 48
Rhymes, skip counting 53
Rhythm 54
Riddles 67, 139–141
Rocks, letter and number 70–74
Roll to Twenty game 35, 36
Root words 92
Rounding 112–113
Running totals 113

S
Safety considerations:
  and planning/preparation 17–18
  strangers 139
  when using sticks 156

Sand tables 214

Scale 122, 191–192

Scavenger hunt, for seeds 179–180

Schedules, outdoor classroom 19–22

Schoolyards 34–104

  activities in 93–104

  learning games in 51–68

  learning tips for 36, 38, 40, 78, 82, 94, 100

  using chalk in 34–51

  using natural materials in 68–93

  as zone of accessibility 4–7, 13

Science activities:

  attracting birds 94–96

  bird talk 182–184

  calculating water in snow 100–102

  designing playgrounds 96–97

  identifying tracks 172–174

  insect inventories 180–182

  investigating snowflakes 99–100

  leaf guides 123–125

  natural materials for 215

  observing bird behavior 184–186

  physics on the playground 97–99

  plant classification 177–179

  in schoolyards 93–102

  seeds scavenger hunt 179–180

  track casting 186–189

Scoot game 57–58

Scrambled words activity 67

Seasons, learning about 200–202

Seating options, outdoor 15

Seeds, activities using 170–172, 179–180

Self-portraits 208–210

Semantics 67–68

Senses, learning about 136

Sensory 44, 100, 215. *See also* Writing activities

Sensory activity 215

Sentence activity 73, 76

Sentences 66–68

Sequencing 65–67

Settings 137–138, 175–177, 195

Shapes 57, 80–81, 109, 110, 150

Sight words, *see* High-frequency words

Silence, variation of math-fact toss up 57

Silly sentence activity 73, 76

Similes 170

Simple machines activity 98

Sit spots 189–196

Skip counting 36, 38, 52–54, 76–78, 114–116

Sledding races 161–164

Snow, activities using 58–59, 81, 82, 87–88, 99–100, 164–167

Snowy conditions, learning tips for 94

Social-emotional needs 2, 10

Sorting activities 66–67, 70, 74–76, 88, 119, 177

Soto, Gary 147

Sound boxes 72

Sounds, activities to learn 61, 72, 119. *See also* Phonemes

Spaces, outdoor classroom 14–15

Spatial reasoning skills activity 121–123

Species, learning about 95, 169
Speed activity 164
Spelling 48–50, 59–65, 67–68, 72
Spirals 109
Stairs, activities using 54, 116, 117
Standardized test scores 3
Starting point experiment 98
Sticks, activities using 76–81, 156
Stick safety 156
Storyboards 50–51
Story elements 51
Storytelling 102–104, 137–138,
      164, 166, 172–174, 186, 195
Street art 48–49
Street names activity 119
Stress, reducing 2, 190
Subitizing activities 57, 72, 79
Subtraction activities 36–38,
      74, 77, 86
Suffixes, activities to learn 92
Summaries 51, 217
Supply lists:
   of natural materials 69
   for outdoor learning 31–33
Support, for outdoor learning
      16–17
Surface area 88
Syllables 60–62, 90
Symmetry 83, 110, 111

T
Temperature 203
Ten frames math activity
      35–37, 82
"Ten ways" activity 145–146
3D models 122–123
3D shapes in snow activity 87–88
Three-layer rule 24, 27–28
Tic-tac-toe word game 59–60

Time, learning about 74, 113,
      200–202
Timelines, historical 66, 145
Time management 19–21
Tourism agencies activity 141–143
Tours, tree 133–134
Tracks, using 95, 172–174, 186–189
Trees 123–134
   books about 129
   inventorying 130–132
   and leaf guide activity 123–125
   leaf resources 125
   locations for using 131
   as overlooked resource
      105–106
   and tree arborists/experts 130
   and tree tours activity 133–134
   utilizing stumps of 6
Trundle wheels 117

U
Urban schools 4–6, 105

V
Verb forms 46
Visual checklists 26
Visual impairments, and sit spots
      190–191
Vocabulary 48–50, 65–67
Voices, community 131
Volume 87–88, 100–102, 164–167

W
Wainwright, Alfred 21
Walking adventures 106–135
   for math 106–117
   for reading and writing 117–123
   and utilizing trees 123–134
Wall displays, about trees 132

War, learning about 145
Water, activity using 100–102
Watercolor art 161
Water tables 214
Weather:
    gear for 21, 28–29
    and outdoor meeting areas
        13–14, 94
    station 97
    tracking 202–204
Wet conditions 28, 94
Wild seed catalogs 170–172
Wind speed, tracking 203–204
Winter, outdoor instruction during
    100, 196
Words:
    activities to learn 118–119
    game using playground 65–67
    high-frequency words 48–50,
        59–62, 67, 73
    marking up 72
    in neighborhoods 118–119
    reading 65–67
    scrambling 73
    to show importance 145
    sorting 119
    tic-tac-toe games using
        59–60
    writing 4
Word graffiti 48–50
Word ladders 46–48
Word problems 43, 58
Word squares 44–46
Work, documenting outdoor 38
Writing:
    descriptive 136
    expository 177

free 137–138
narrative 202
portable surfaces for 107
procedural 103–104
Writing activities. *See also* Reading
    and writing activities
    cloud stories 102–104
    descriptive writing 136
    imagining what is behind
        doors 139
    leaf guide 123
    nature riddles 139–141
    neighborhood odes 147,
        148–149
    neighborhoods as setting
        137–138
    news, sit spot 193–195
    personification 146
    procedural writing 103–104
    "ten ways" versions 145–146
    tourism agencies 141–143
    for utilizing schoolyards
        102–104

Y
Year-end reflections 209
Yearlong projects 205–217
    class nature journals 205–208
    natural materials for 214–215
    nature collections 210–213
    observing trees 125–129
    phenology wheels 215–217
    self-portraits 208–210
    sit spots 189–196

Z
Zones of accessibility 4–11